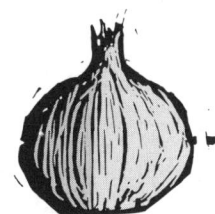

ENVIRONMENTAL ACTION
Analyze **C**onsider options **T**ake action **I**n **O**ur **N**eighborhoods

FOOD
Choices

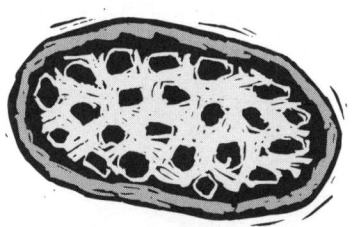

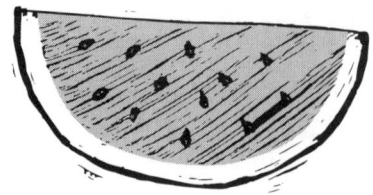

A Student Audit of Resource Use

TEACHER RESOURCE GUIDE

E2: ENVIRONMENT & EDUCATION

DALE SEYMOUR PUBLICATIONS®
WHITE PLAINS, NEW YORK

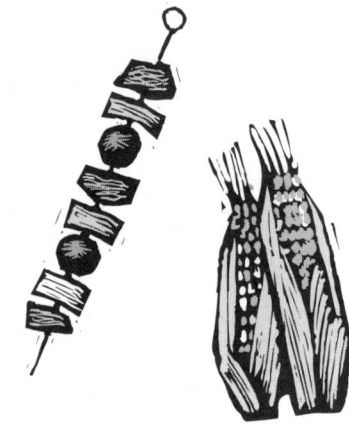

Developed by E2: Environment & Education™, an activity of the Tides Center.

Managing Editor: Cathy Anderson
Senior Editor: Jeri Hayes
Production/Manufacturing Director: Janet Yearian
Design Manager: Jeff Kelly
Senior Production Coordinator: Fiona Santoianni
Text and Cover Design: Lynda Banks Design
Art: Rachel Gage, Andrea Reider
Composition: Andrea Reider
Clip Art Illustrations Copyright © Art Parts, Courtesy Art Parts, 714-834-9166
Contributing Writers: Susan Blackaby and Jane Van Dusen

This book is published by Dale Seymour Publications®,
an imprint of Addison Wesley Longman, Inc.

Dale Seymour Publications
10 Bank Street
White Plains, NY 10602
Customer Service: 800-872-1100

Copyright © 1998 The Tides Center/E2: Environment & Education
All rights reserved.
Printed in the United States of America.

Limited reproduction permission: The publisher grants permission to individual teachers who have purchased this book to reproduce the blackline masters as needed for use with their own students. Reproduction for an entire school or school district or for commercial use is prohibited.

Printed on acid-free, 85% recycled paper (15% post-consumer), using soy-based ink.

ISBN 0-201-49530-9
DS36858
1 2 3 4 5 6 7 8 9 10-ML-01 00 99 98 97

ACKNOWLEDGMENTS

Tom and Rampa Hormel, Christopher and Luanne Hormel, Angela Hormel Ocone, and Diane Ives from the Global Environment Project Institute (GEPI) for their unwavering support in developing this action program for students

Jay Dean Paschall of Global Learning and Observation to Benefit the Environment (GLOBE) for developing the concept for this program (originally called EarthTime)

Human-i-Tees for generous support of the review and pilot school portion of the program

The Center for Environmental Education for use of their resource materials

Leslie Crawford for writing and producing *Environmental ACTION*

EarthTime Contributors

Larry J. Barnes, Ketchum, ID
Betty Bell, Ketchum, ID
J. B. Burrell, Ketchum, ID
Scott Graves, T.R.E.E., Boise, ID
Irene S. Healy, Wood River High School, Hailey, ID
Carrie Hislaire, Sun Valley, ID
Michelle Richer, Ketchum, ID
Doug Wilson, Ketchum, ID

Environmental ACTION Contributors

Martin J. Byhower, Chadwick School, Palos Verdes, CA
Jennifer Daza, E2: Environment & Education
Bruce Harlan, St. Matthew's Parish School, Pacific Palisades, CA
Anne Kirstin Holm, student at Yale University
Laura Jean Moore, San Diego, CA
Bonnie Slagel, Los Angeles, CA

Pilot School Participants

Michele Cheyne, Hamilton High School, Milwaukee, WI
Neil Coen, East Magnet School, Kansas City, MO
Steve Engleman, Paul Revere Middle School, Los Angeles, CA
Leroy Hickerson, Alcee Fortier Senior High School, New Orleans, LA
Stephen Hopkins, Sly Park Environmental Education Center, Pollack Pines, CA
Dick Jordan, Boise High School, Boise, ID
Donna Gross McDaniel, Alcee Fortier Senior High School, New Orleans, LA
Dennis Pilien, Bravo Medical Magnet, Los Angeles, CA
Scott Sala, Cory Elementary School, Denver, CO
Pat Shepard, Miller-South School for Visual and Performing Arts, Akron, OH

Educational Reviewers

Karl Abrahms, Saddleback College, Mission Viejo, CA
Tammy Bird, Crenshaw High School, Los Angeles, CA
Alison L. Brown, Beekmantown Central School, Plattsburgh, NY
Martin Byhower, Chadwick School, Palos Verdes, CA
Joan Grimm, Department of Environmental Quality, Portland, OR
Bruce Harlan, St. Matthew's Parish School, Pacific Palisades, CA
Kay Ice, Educational Development Specialists, Lakewood, CA
Kurt Leuschner, Mira Costa High School, Manhattan Beach, CA
Stephanie Wald, Allan Hancock College, Santa Maria, CA

Professional Reviewers

Christopher Balthasar, EarthSave Foundation, Santa Monica, CA
Mari Clements, Nutrition Information Center, Crozer-Chester Medical Center, Upland, PA
Wayne R. Gould, Southern California Edison, Rosemead, CA
Joe Haworth, Sanitation Districts of Los Angeles County, Whittier, CA
Richard Heede, Rocky Mountain Institute, Snowmass, CO
Steven Hulbert, Saturn of Olympia, Olympia, WA
Sherman Morrison, North American Coalition on Religion and Ecology, Washington, DC
Gary Petersen, Recycle America, Los Angeles, CA

E2 Board of Advisors

Peter Corcoran, Bates College
Irene Healy, Wood River High School
Christopher Hormel, Global Environment Project Institute (GEPI)
Rampa Hormel, GEPI
Tom Hormel, GEPI
Dean Paschall, Global Learning and Observation to Benefit the Environment (GLOBE)
Drummond Pike, Tides Foundation and Tides Center

CONTENTS

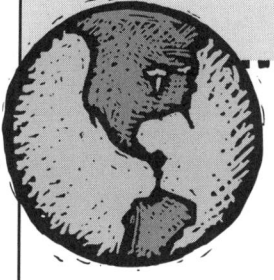

Welcome to Environmental ACTION!

About the Environmental ACTION Program	3
Program Mission and Objectives	3
Program Description	4
Program Components	5
Moving Through a Module	6
Teaching Environmental ACTION	8
Community Involvement	9
Cooperative Learning	10
What's Next?	13
Environmental ACTION Feedback	13
About This Module	14
Teaching *Food Choices*	14
Assessment Tools	16
Cross-Curricular Suggestions	17

EXPLORE the Issues

Investigate Foods and the Environment	21
Activity Sheet 1: Food Production and the Environment	24
Use the Food Guide Pyramid	26
Activity Sheet 2: The Food Guide Pyramid	30
Evaluate Nutritional Values	32
Activity Sheet 3: Food Labels	34
Practice Making Food Choices	36
Activity Sheet 4: Choosing Foods	39

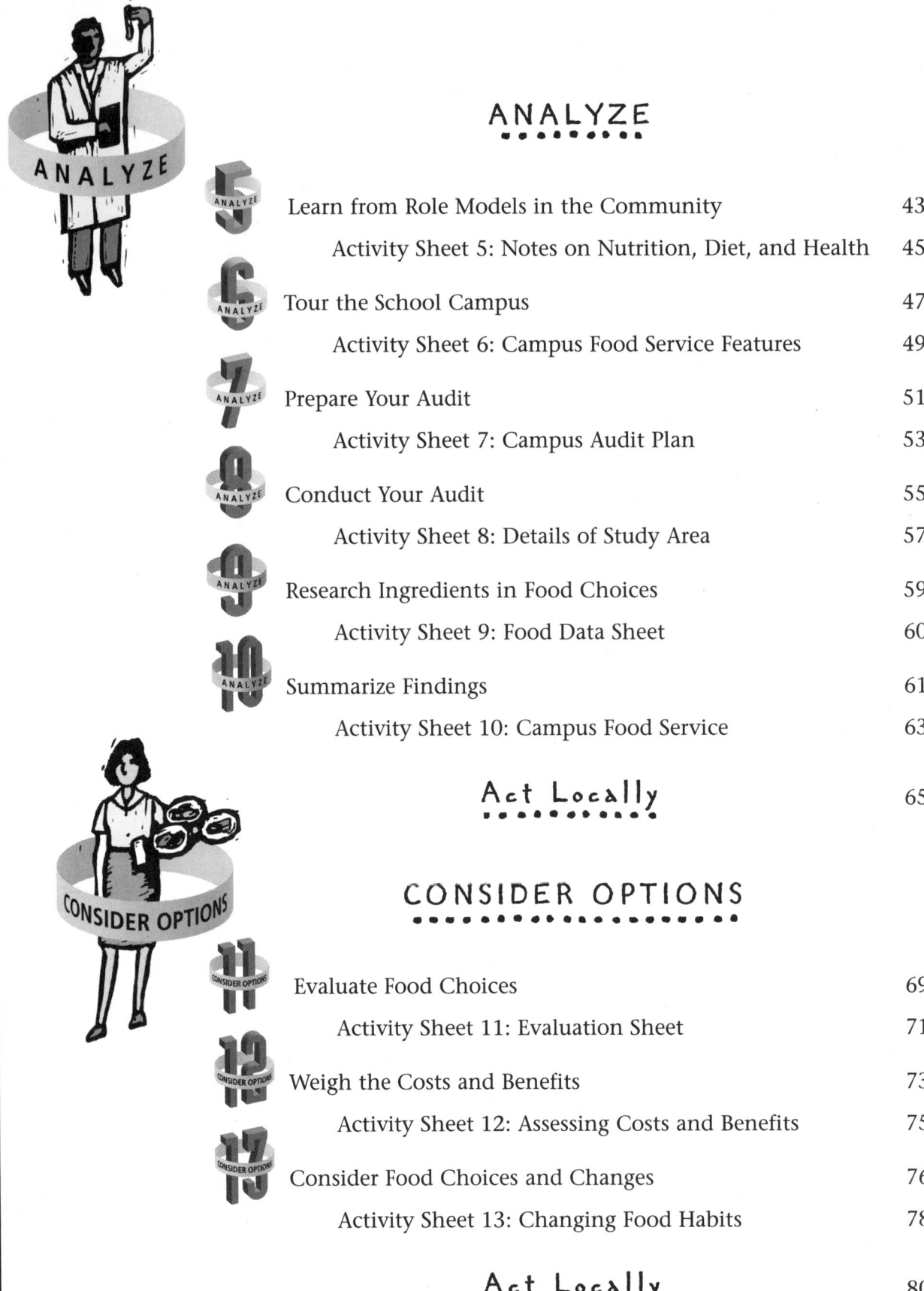

ANALYZE

Learn from Role Models in the Community	43
Activity Sheet 5: Notes on Nutrition, Diet, and Health	45
Tour the School Campus	47
Activity Sheet 6: Campus Food Service Features	49
Prepare Your Audit	51
Activity Sheet 7: Campus Audit Plan	53
Conduct Your Audit	55
Activity Sheet 8: Details of Study Area	57
Research Ingredients in Food Choices	59
Activity Sheet 9: Food Data Sheet	60
Summarize Findings	61
Activity Sheet 10: Campus Food Service	63

Act Locally — 65

CONSIDER OPTIONS

Evaluate Food Choices	69
Activity Sheet 11: Evaluation Sheet	71
Weigh the Costs and Benefits	73
Activity Sheet 12: Assessing Costs and Benefits	75
Consider Food Choices and Changes	76
Activity Sheet 13: Changing Food Habits	78

Act Locally — 80

TAKE ACTION

Food Choice Recommendations	83
Activity Sheet 14: Rating Sheet	85
Prepare and Present Proposal	86
Activity Sheet 15: Proposal Checklist	88
Track Responses to Recommendations	90
Activity Sheet 16: Tracking Sheet	92

Appendices

Issues and Information

Section A	Food Production Practices and the Environment	97
Section B	The Food Guide Pyramid	100
Section C	Nutrition Basics	103
Section D	How to Read Food Labels	108
Section E	Knowing What Is Good for You	111
Section F	What You Can Do: Making Food Choices That Are Healthy for the Environment	115

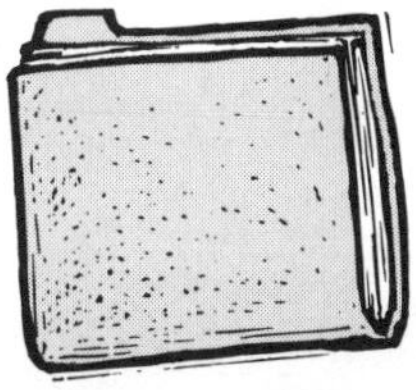

Glossary	116
Teacher Resources	117
Organizations	119
Government Agencies	123
Books and Pamphlets	124
Magazines and Newsletters	126
Products and Services	127

Blackline Masters

Activity Sheets — 131

Assessment Tools
- Content Quiz — 160
- Student Survey — 162
- Student Self-Evaluation Form — 163
- Action Group Evaluation Form — 164
- Program Evaluation Form — 165

Welcome to Environmental ACTION!

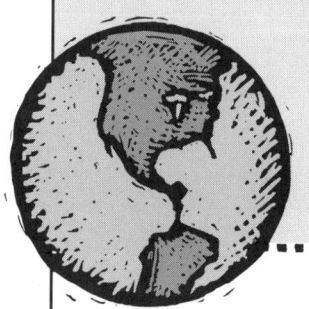

About the Environmental ACTION Program

As the natural resources crisis reaches global proportions—air, water, and land pollution; limited supplies of fossil fuels; threatened and endangered habitats; species facing extinction—people must acknowledge the enormous role that they have played in creating or exacerbating the problems and the enormous role they can potentially play to alter the course of events. As educators, we feel it is vital to give students the information and skills they will need in order to take action. We need to help students learn to look critically at environmental issues and take personal responsibility for finding solutions by asking questions: What is the problem? What causes the problem? What impact does behavior have on the problem? What changes can be made or actions taken to help? By introducing an action-based curriculum, we not only begin preparing the next generation for dealing with difficult issues, we teach students how to live healthier lives in the process.

The school is an ideal laboratory for this hands-on experiment because it provides a real-world model. Students gather information about the school, analyze environmental issues within the context of the information gathered, determine positive alternatives, and practice implementing solutions right in the school setting. For example, students may decide that by using energy-efficient lighting, implementing water conservation programs, moving toward environment-friendly landscaping, or using nontoxic chemicals to clean and maintain facilities, they can improve the school environment, reduce resource use, and perhaps even save money. They present their proposal for changes to the school for approval. If the changes are implemented, the school then becomes a useful living paradigm; students can participate in and observe the changes, monitor results, and extend their knowledge to their own homes. It is this learning/doing, school/community partnership that makes Environmental ACTION a unique environmental education curriculum.

Program Mission and Objectives

Environmental ACTION was developed in response to the need for environmental education materials that emphasize personal responsibility and positive action. The program's mission is to empower students with the knowledge and skills necessary to make meaningful changes that can be carried into the future. Many educators have been challenged to find appropriate materials and the necessary teaching support to offer this kind of environmental education to their students. Environmental ACTION meets these needs by providing a relevant, supportive, clearly structured curriculum specifically aimed at middle and secondary students.

The six modules in the program provide step-by-step instruction on how to investigate real-world environmental issues and present opportunities to learn and practice action skills in the context of these issues. By creating a laboratory within the school community, the program gives students the opportunity to learn and develop personal responsibility through practical application.

The curriculum has the following objectives:

- to promote awareness of environmental issues through real-world investigations
- to build the knowledge and skills needed to analyze, investigate, and offer solutions to environmental problems

- to encourage practical application of knowledge and skills in issue resolution
- to assist students in becoming responsible citizens by involving them in the extended school community

Program Description

The program consists of six modules designed for use in middle and secondary schools. Each module includes a Teacher Resource Guide and Student Edition. Following is a brief description of the six modules:

Energy Conservation
Students explore the sources, production, uses, and environmental effects of energy. They apply their learning by examining ways to improve the energy efficiency of their school and homes.

Food Choices
Students investigate the effects of food production, diet, and nutrition on human health and the environment. Students analyze the school's food service program to identify healthy choices and practices.

Habitat and Biodiversity
Students study the importance of biological diversity, landscape management, xeriscaping, composting, and integrated pest management (IPM). Using the school as a research laboratory, students assess the current landscaping, then evaluate its present health and environmental impact. This module also contains a step-by-step guide to creating an organic garden and seed bank.

Chemicals: Choosing Wisely
Students investigate the types of materials, chemical products, cleaning supplies, and pesticides used in their school—how they are used, stored, and disposed of, and their potential effects on human health and the environment. Students develop a plan for implementing Earth- and human-friendly alternatives for school and home.

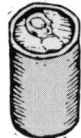

Waste Reduction
Students sort and analyze school garbage to identify recyclable and compostable materials. They formulate a plan to reduce their consumption and waste at school and at home, including developing a recycling program or improving an existing one.

Water Conservation
After an introduction to water consumption and quality issues, students conduct an audit of water usage and efficiency on the school campus. Using the school as a research laboratory, students develop strategies for implementing water conservation at school and at home.

Options for Using the Program

These six modules are part of a complete yet flexible curriculum package. Because they are designed to be used either in conjunction with one another or as stand-alone units, a variety of teaching options are offered. For example, one module can be taught year after year, different modules can be taught in consecutive years, or different modules can be taught in a given year. Modules may be taught by a team, or a group of teachers may choose to simultaneously present different modules.

Using the Program Outside School

In response to a growing number of requests, Environmental ACTION has been designed for use by groups that operate outside a formal school setting. Issue investigation and action activities in the Teacher Resource Guide and Student Edition can be easily adapted to fit different venues and circumstances. For example, an ecology club might use the program at a school, community center, or local business; church groups can use it to explore their stewardship responsibilities within the church community or as an outreach project; community-based organizations can conduct the activities at their centers as part of their efforts to improve the quality of life within the local community. Wherever choices are made with respect to natural resource consumption, there exists an opportunity for investigation, evaluation, and action—and Environmental ACTION can provide a framework for these efforts.

Program Components

Each module consists of a Student Edition and a Teacher Resource Guide that complement one another and provide maximum flexibility for teachers.

Student Edition

Each activity is presented using a clear and consistent format that puts students in charge of their own learning. Setting the Stage offers discussion questions that will pique students' interest and direct their attention to the objectives of the lesson. Vocabulary is included as appropriate. The Focus part of the activity provides the core of the lesson, leading students through a step-by-step process. Central to this section is an activity sheet, which can be duplicated for students to complete individually or in groups. (Blackline masters for all activity sheets are located at the back of the Teacher Resource Guide.) It's a Wrap reviews student work and provides closure to the activity. The Home activity allows students to apply their learning outside the school environment.

Teacher Resource Guide

The material in the Teacher Resource Guide duplicates key text in the Student Edition—questions, assignments, and activity sheets. Concepts and objectives are itemized, special vocabulary is listed, and student responses are suggested. Activity sheets in the Teacher Resource Guide include annotated answers. The Teacher Resource Guide contains the same Issues and Information section and Glossary that appear in the Student Edition, along with some additional resources and assessment tools. The blackline masters for all activity sheets are located at the end of the Teacher Resource Guide.

Moving Through a Module

Each activity within a module is a separate lesson, and most are designed to take only one class period. The program consists of four types of activities: Explore the Issues, Analyze, Consider Options, and Take Action. The teaching methodology, illustrated below, presents activities in a sequence that first introduces students to global environmental issues, then requires them to apply critical thinking skills to environmental issues in their immediate environment, and finally encourages them to take responsibility through independent action.

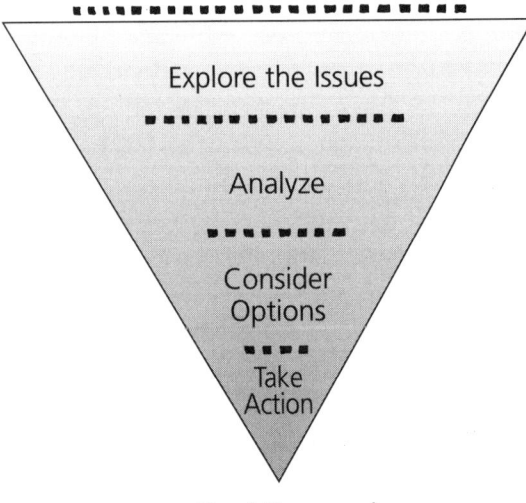

Explore the Issues Activities

In the first four activities in each module, students are given an overview of the environmental topics that pertain to the issues they will focus on in their investigation of school, home, and community. The Explore the Issues activities gives students opportunities to gather information and build environmental awareness. Students will work individually, in small groups, and as a class.

ACT Activities

The remaining activities are structured to provide an environment for students to move from awareness to choice to action. The three-part teaching sequence—ACT—reflects the following process:
- Analyze
- Consider Options
- Take Action

Analyze Activities Students focus their attention on the school campus or other facility. Working in small groups, students develop and implement a plan for collecting and recording data. Finally, students identify environmental, financial, and human health costs and benefits of current school practices affecting, for example, energy use, waste disposal, or whatever topic is the focus of the particular module.

Consider Options Activities Students investigate alternative practices, services, technologies, and products. Then they evaluate each on a costs/benefits basis, using material in the Issues and Information section at the back of the book.

Take Action Activities Based on the options that students have discovered, groups of students recommend changes in practices and products. The class then discusses and evaluates the recommendations and ultimately reaches a consensus as to which recommendations to propose to the school administration or environmental committee. (Note: See Community Recognition, p. 9, for further discussion on local outreach.) The closing activities involve writing the proposal. This final step in each Environmental ACTION module is intended to launch students on a course for creating a healthier and more balanced environment.

Home

Each activity includes ideas for parallel investigations and analysis that students can do at home. These activities reinforce the learning going on at school and provide an opportunity for students to apply the knowledge to practices and choices made at home. Family members may also choose to get involved. The Home activities are optional; they are not required for the completion of the school environmental audit or other activities within the module. We suggest that students' Home assignments be written in a Journal. (See Student Journals, below.)

Act Locally

In order to effect meaningful change in areas related to human health and the environment, it is essential that students practice taking action. As with other areas of learning, practicing a behavior makes it grow into habit. Therefore, Act Locally activities—straightforward outreach projects to present to the school or community—are provided for use after the Analyze and Consider Options sections. Students can choose to implement one of the suggested activities or develop an activity of their own. In either case, these Act Locally activities serve as opportunities for students to practice putting their ideas into action.

Student Journals

Student work on the Home assignments at the end of each activity can be recorded in student Journals, along with notes, sketches, data collection, and other student writing that takes place during the module. Journals may be kept private and used for referral and note-taking during discussions, or they may be used to record answers to specific questions in the Focus or It's a Wrap sections. Since some Journal material may be turned in and some kept for personal use only, a loose-leaf notebook or folder is an ideal choice.

You may want to extend the use of the Journal by suggesting additional writing assignments that call on students to make observations about what they have noted, synthesize or analyze the data, compare and contrast information, draw conclusions, or make generalizations. All of these activities provide opportunities for students to use critical thinking skills and communicate ideas—valuable experiences for most middle and high school students. Additional ideas for Journal assignments can be found in the Cross-Curricular Activities Chart for the module. (See Cross-Curricular Suggestions, below.)

Issues and Information

An Issues and Information appendix appears in both the Student Edition and the Teacher Resource Guide. This appendix contains a variety of materials students need to complete the activities and develop a deeper understanding of the issues they are studying. The appendix is divided into easily accessible sections and, in some modules, may be accompanied by illustrations.

Cross-Curricular Suggestions

At the end of the introductory material for each module, you will find specific suggestions for cross-curricular activities and extensions in the following content areas: history/social studies, language arts, math, and science. These suggestions offer opportunities to extend study activities to higher cognitive skill levels and/or to meet your school's curriculum framework with activities that link directly to specific components.

Teaching Environmental ACTION

Scheduling and Managing Modules Start a module with enough time—18–20 class sessions—for students to conduct research and implement changes. Since students will be needing activity sheets for all the activities, you may wish to photocopy them before starting a module. The blackline masters are located at the end of the Teacher Resource Guide. Before starting the first activity, introduce students to the project, administer the Content Quiz and Student Survey provided in the Blackline Masters/Assessment Tools section, and familiarize students with the Student Edition. You may also wish to have students write to agencies, organizations, manufacturers, and businesses (listed in the Teacher Resources section of the Teacher Resource Guide) in order to obtain materials and request information that can be used as the module progresses. Once the students are working in their Action Groups to investigate and analyze their subjects, additional research time outside of the actual class sessions may need to be scheduled.

Skipping or Modifying Activities Since all of the activities have been carefully designed to help students build their investigation of the school environment, we encourage you to complete each activity. If you do omit or modify an activity, be sure that students incorporate the activity's objectives into the project. You may be able to teach or facilitate your students' comprehension of a learning objective in a different way or combine activities in order to make sure that your students do not miss meaningful steps in the discovery process.

The Teacher's Role The Environmental ACTION modules are activity driven. The scope and sequence has been designed carefully so that the transition from teacher- to student-directed activities happens gradually and within well-outlined parameters. In the beginning, you will be in the more traditional role of the teacher, providing information and leading the students through the Explore the Issues activities. As the class begins the ACT activities, you will assume the role of facilitator for your students' efforts.

Small group work will be the activity most likely to affect your role in relation to the students. Although you will continue to supervise them, you will not be directing their work. Students working in Action Groups will be responsible for keeping on task, catching their mistakes, supporting each other, and meeting their goals. Students may not always carry out their work in a way that you would have directed, but this learning process allows them to make mistakes and correct their actions.

As your students work through the actual audit and your role becomes more that of a facilitator, your responsibilities may include some or all of the following:

- serving as liaison between the students and the school administration
- keeping the students' work on schedule
- monitoring the groups' interactions
- advising Action Groups about procedures and resources and assisting with problem-solving
- reserving reference and resource books in the school library or classroom for student research

Toward the end of the ACT sequence, students will meet again as a class to finalize their proposal. At this point, you will evaluate the group dynamics of your students and assess the degree of facilitation necessary. After students write the proposal and present it to the school administration or environmental committee, the actual implementation steps will be determined by the school's willingness to take action and your students' commitment to the project.

Student Project Coordinator To provide more leadership opportunities, you may wish to create the role of Project Coordinator for one student or several students. The Project Coordinator can volunteer, can be appointed by you, can be selected by the class, or can be chosen at random to assist you with the administration and facilitation of the project in the following ways:

- Lead large group sessions
- Serve as liaison between the Action Groups and you or the class and the school administration
- Help to monitor and keep Action Groups on schedule
- Oversee the preparation and distribution of materials, including activity sheets

Community Involvement

Community Participation The Environmental ACTION modules enable students to participate in community service activities and help students develop a commitment to public service. For optimum success, you and your students will want to cultivate the goodwill of all potential participants from the beginning of the project. These participants may include other students, teachers, administrators, librarians, kitchen staff, custodians, maintenance staff, and purchasing personnel, as well as members of the community. The following are some hints that may be helpful in gaining the participation and cooperation of members of your community:

- Notify key support groups in your school and community of your project.
- Provide all participants with a description of the activities and a description of things students will be doing in the course of their work.
- Make a formal request for any specific considerations or resources needed from these individuals.
- Inform students' parents. They may be able to contribute additional resources and/or expertise. Also, parents' understanding of homework assignments such as the home audits will help ensure a positive and productive experience.
- Recognize the cultural, economic, and ethnic diversity of your school community and be sensitive to the varied perceptions of issues related to human health and the health of the environment.

Community Recognition It is important for the students to realize that their responsible investigations of an environmental issue and development of a logical plan for taking action have earned serious consideration by the community. Therefore, it is critical to engage community involvement that will include a thoughtful response to the students' final report and proposal.

One way to encourage community participation is to create an environmental committee at your school. This committee can be set up at the beginning of the project. The members may include parents, teachers, students, administrators, and other school staff. If a school Ecology Club is already in place, you may wish to explore establishing a committee under the auspices of the club. The committee can serve as a resource, a liaison between the students and school officials, and a review body for ideas and suggestions for implementing changes. In order to be effective, the committee will probably need to meet periodically throughout the project to hear status reports and to respond to requests for assistance or advice. You may want to draft a written agreement detailing the role of participants and the service each agrees to provide.

Recognition of students' efforts to bring about positive change in the school setting could include a public award ceremony, certificates of merit, academic or extra-curricular credit, or establishment of an Implementation Committee on which students might serve.

Bringing Role Models into the Classroom

The first activity in each Analyze section suggests that you ask leaders from your community or resource people who are familiar with the school to present information related to the module issue. Plan ahead to find and make arrangements for guest speakers. It can be a time-consuming task, but outside participation in this project is important for a number of reasons:

- The information provided will help students understand how the issue relates to their community, school, family, and themselves.
- Students will be able to ask questions and obtain answers that will assist them in their investigation and audit of the school campus.
- Role models from your community can become valuable and accessible resources for you and your students.

What kinds of role models make effective guest speakers? The main criterion is that they are familiar with the module issue. You may want to invite a school administrator, parent, elected official, resource person with a government agency or advocacy organization, business owner, medical professional, or a family member of one of your students. Your students may have some good ideas about whom they would like to meet and hear speak. You might invite a number of guests to allow students to hear several points of view.

A fun and interactive way to present a speaker is to introduce the guest to your students without revealing the person's connection to the module issue. Then play Twenty Questions, having students ask yes/no questions to try to discover the person's role. Once the role is determined or the maximum number of questions has been asked, you can introduce the guest and provide some background.

Cooperative Learning

Cooperative learning—including small-group discussion, problem-solving, and decision-making activities—is an integral part of the Environmental ACTION curriculum. Because some students may not have previous experience with these processes or may not yet have developed strong skills, you may need to prepare them for this type of interaction. The effectiveness of small group discussion as a learning tool varies widely according to several fairly concrete parameters, and you can influence the outcome in your classroom by sharing these with your students, thus providing a model for them to work toward.

First, we believe that small group discussion is most effective when the number of participants is limited (four to six) to allow members to be aware of and react to one another. Additionally, it is critical that participants have a common understanding of goal(s), have a sense of being part of the group and are willing to work cooperatively, work toward open dialogue and discussion among participants, and recognize that individual accomplishment depends upon the group's success.

Following are some questions and answers about basic cooperative learning terminology and ways to manage small group experiences. Many of these topics are discussed in more detail in *Effective Group Discussion* by John K. Brilhart (Wm. C. Brown Company Publishers, Dubuque, Iowa).

Q: What makes an effective Action Group member?
A: Characteristics include a sense of responsibility for helping the group accomplish its objectives, active participation, willingness to accept tasks, and commitment to the group through good and bad. Also, effective group members offer positive feedback on ideas and information, avoid using words that induce negative feelings, make organized comments, speak concisely, state one point at a time, pose specific questions, and listen courteously and attentively. It is to be expected that students will improve their skills in these areas as they gain experience working in their Action Group.

Roles for individual group members will evolve through the workings of the group. In some cases, there may be no apparent leader but lots of leadership. Conversely, groups may have leaders but lack direction. The best-case scenario is for each group to have a leader who oversees procedures and facilitates the group's process.

Q: How should Action Groups be organized physically?
A: Action Groups work best when they are in comfortable environments that do not offer a lot of distractions. Students should sit close together in a circle and have access to writing surfaces. If you notice some awkwardness when students are first assigned to Action Groups, you might want to introduce an ice-breaker activity to help them get comfortable with working together.

Q: What can I expect from students working in Action Groups?
A: Small groups usually progress through several steps before achieving end goals. Groups vary in terms of the time it takes to move through some or all of the following steps:

- Members of the group work to develop a cohesiveness of goals and understanding of one another.
- The group establishes the identities and roles of individual members, including leadership roles. This step may be accompanied by disagreements.
- The group finds ways to manage disagreements by establishing rules and procedural standards. This usually results in more agreement and an increased feeling of freedom to offer opinions and have them heard.
- The group focuses on the goal(s), and discussion is concentrated on developing solutions to the problems identified.

Q: Is decision-making the same as problem-solving?
A: No. Problem-solving involves a number of phases—identifying the problem; investigating alternatives; developing an implementation plan; and making the necessary changes. Problem-solving sessions should focus on the issue and a careful framing of the problem question before discussing possible solutions. They should also encourage participants to share their knowledge about the issue and refrain from making judgments when discussing alternatives. Decision-making comes into the problem-solving process whenever students choose between various options or possible courses of action.

Q: When is group brainstorming an appropriate process?
A: Brainstorming is an appropriate small group discussion tool when a number of solutions exist for a particular problem. The following conditions of brainstorming should be communicated to participants before brainstorming sessions begin:

- Any idea is valid; the more, the merrier.
- Ideas can build upon previous suggestions.
- Suggestions should not be judged until brainstorming has ended.

Q: What is consensus decision-making?
A: Consensus decision-making is an alternative to the more traditional majority vote group decision-making. In the consensus process, value is placed on each member of the group agreeing to a decision. It may not be the preferred decision of any individual, but it is something everyone can live with. This type of decision-making allows for the group to meet a multitude of criteria for making a choice and for each member to derive satisfaction from the final result. However, consensus decision-making can take considerably longer than other processes such as voting, and in some cases it is not feasible to achieve total agreement.

If you choose to make use of consensus decision-making, you may want to follow certain steps. First, list options, stating reasons in favor of and against them. Next, rank options according to criteria such as accessibility or time constraints. Then, consolidate ideas and summarize the class discussion. Next, narrow down the options to one or two. Using the chalkboard, you might list under each option the pros and cons. Ask for a class vote. If the vote is not unanimous, ask volunteers for each side to explain their reasons. Encourage students to use persuasive arguments but also to listen attentively to the opposing arguments. Continue polling the class until finally all are in agreement about their choice of a study area. Activity sheets are provided for this purpose.

Q: If an Action Group is not staying focused, what can I do?
A: You can help by asking one or more of the following questions:

What are you meeting about? What is your common goal? What do you want to achieve as a group? Are you staying on track with your tasks?

Evaluating Students' Work

There are numerous ways to evaluate students' work and progress. We suggest you begin with the Student Survey provided in the Blackline Masters/Assessment Tools section at the end of this book. This survey contains both objective and subjective questions and can be given at the beginning and the end of the project. If used at the beginning, the process of reviewing the students' answers can serve as a device for discussion or as a tool for assessing your students' base level of knowledge about a particular issue. If used again at the end of the project, the survey can help you evaluate the amount of learning and changed attitudes/behaviors that resulted from students' investigations and activities.

To evaluate different aspects of an individual student's participation in the Action Groups, you may choose to use the Action Group Evaluation Form. This is a simple checklist for your reference. The blackline master is provided in the Assessment Tools section on page 164 of this book. Another evaluation tool that works well in a cooperative setting is a self-evaluation submitted by students. A blackline master Student Self-Evaluation Form is provided on page 163 of the Assessment Tools section. In order to best assess long-term performance, you will want to schedule evaluations at regular intervals throughout the project.

What's Next?

Teachers often wonder what happens after their class completes a module and initiates changes or environmental activities at the school. What is next semester's or next year's class supposed to do? As long as the school has areas that need improvement, learning opportunities abound. The following are some options you may find useful:

- Repeat the module activities to evaluate the impact of changes, and continue to develop additional recommendations including modifications of the previous changes.
- Maintain the newly instituted activities at the school.
- Choose another module, and allow your students to explore a different environmental issue.

Environmental ACTION Feedback

We are interested in the ongoing short- and long-term effects of implementing our curriculum at schools, so we invite you to provide feedback about your experience. The data collected will not only provide us with information about the effectiveness of the curriculum, it will allow us to compile information illustrating the degree of change occurring on campuses nationally and abroad. This information also becomes a peer-networking resource for teachers and students who have questions about implementing environmental programs at their schools. We ask that you take a few minutes at the conclusion of this project to complete the Program Evaluation Form located at the end of this guide. We also urge you, at any time, to visit our Web site. The address is: <http://www.enviroaction.org>. Let's share our successes and challenges! We'll add your contribution to our site.

About This Module

Teaching Food Choices

Begin by giving students an overview of the module and its activities. Tell them that this project is aimed at making food choices that are healthy for the body and for the environment Explain that they will be studying different campus sites to audit what foods are offered, how they are prepared and packaged, what nutrients they contain, how they fit into the Food Guide Pyramid, and how they are produced in order to make healthy choices, change bad habits, and suggest alternatives to the food service staff.

Distribute the Student Editions and ask your students to read the Welcome! section. Allow time for discussion of the students books, teacher/student roles, evaluation, schedules, contact with the school administration, procedures, and Student Journals.

To assess students' prior knowledge of this topic before they begin work and to get them thinking critically about making healthy food choices, you may want to have students complete the Student Survey provided in the Blackline Masters/Assessment Tools section of this guide, page 162. (A discussion about using the survey as an assessment tool appears on page 16.)

Since much of the work in this program will be done in small groups, you may want to take time at this point to explain the methodology of Action Groups and to offer tips on how to work cooperatively. (See pages 10–12 for specific suggestions on facilitating Action Groups.)

Time Requirements Most activities are designed to be conducted in a single 50- or 55-minute class session. The first and second Analyze activities may take more than one session, depending on how many guests are invited to speak and how the tours are organized. Also, Action Group work and homework in several of the activities require extra time outside of class. The amount of time assigned to homework and independent group work can vary.

Materials and Preparation Implementation of the *Food Choices* module requires no special materials or equipment. Cookbooks and nutrition guides would be helpful to have on hand. Students will need pencils and paper to take notes and make Journal entries while surveying the school. Poster board, oak tag, construction paper, markers, and general art supplies will help students make effective presentations.

Blackline masters for the activity sheets are located at the end of this book. You may choose to photocopy all of them before beginning a new module, or one at a time at the appropriate point in the lesson. See the Prepare section of each activity for any additional preparation required.

Explore the Issues Activities

The Explore activities emphasize "the big picture," presenting data for students to analyze and use to create diagrams, charts, and graphs, and offering ideas about how responsible individual and/or group action can effect positive environmental change. Students become aware of how food is produced, how food production impacts the environment, guidelines to follow to make healthy choices. The activities give students experience working independently, in small groups, and as a class.

Activity 1: Investigate Foods and the Environment Students will find out about different types of food, factors that affect food production, and ways in which food production can impact the environment.

Activity 2: Use the Food Guide Pyramid The diet that is healthiest for people may also be healthiest for the environment. Students find out what it means to eat a healthy diet by learning about food groups and following the recommendations of the Food Guide Pyramid.

Activity 3: Evaluate Nutritional Values People need to get certain nutrients from their diets in order to be healthy. Americans tend to get too little of some nutrients and too much of some others. Students will learn about nutrients and the guidelines for maintaining good health through a well-balanced diet.

Activity 4: Practice Making Food Choices Making healthy food choices means understanding how food is used by the body to maintain good health. Students will find out more about essential nutrients and the foods that provide them.

ACT Activities

Once students have an overview of how food choices relate to health and to the environment, they embark on the ACT activities. These activities guide students through the process of conducting an audit of the school food service (Analyze activities); investigate food choices (Consider Options activities); and recommend changes in choices and habits (Take Action activities).

Analyze Activities

Activity 5: Learn from Role Models in the Community Students learn about diet and nutrition issues from a community resource person.

Activity 6: Tour the School Campus Students learn about diet and nutrition issues related to food service on the school campus from a resource person. They tour the campus and list information about food sources and preparation, cost, and nutrition considerations.

Activity 7: Prepare Your Audit Using the information collected on Activity Sheet 6 and the campus tour notes, students will divide the campus into study areas for the audit.

Activity 8: Conduct Your Audit Action Groups will investigate their study areas and use their observations to list features related to source, preparation, nutrition, cost.

Activity 9: Research Ingredients in Food Choices Students will research what goes into the foods that are served and identify the nutrients they provide.

Activity 10: Summarize Findings Students will review audit results, evaluate the types of foods that are served, describe their nutritional value, and summarize their findings.

Consider Options Activities

Activity 11: Evaluate Food Choices Students will now begin looking at specific ways to improve the food choices they make. They will first review the reports completed during Activity 10 and then evaluate the food choices at each study area.

Activity 12: Weigh the Costs and Benefits Students will evaluate healthy food choices by analyzing their costs and benefits.

Activity 13: Consider Food Choices and Changes Students have learned about the environmental and health considerations that come into play when making food choices, and they have weighed costs and benefits of each choice. Now they are ready to take all of these things into consideration as they make personal food choices and recommend changes to implement at school.

Take Action Activities

Activity 14: Food Choice Recommendations
Students have explored making healthy food choices, taking into account costs and benefits as well as environmental considerations. Have them work together in their Action Groups to recommend food choice changes they would like to see implemented on campus.

Activity 15: Prepare and Present Proposal
Students will write a proposal for recommending healthy food choices at school. They will outline costs, benefits, and describe the ways to implement their recommendations. Then they will present the proposal to the school committee.

Activity 16: Track Response to Recommendations
Students will follow up on their healthy food choice proposal as it is implemented on campus. They will work to increase awareness of nutrition and environmental considerations in order to begin changing the habits of the student body and staff.

Assessment Tools

The following assessment tools have been provided in the Blackline Master/Assessment Tools section of this guide: Content Quiz, Student Survey, Student Self-Evaluation Form, and Action Group Evaluation Form. At this time you may wish to administer the Content Quiz and the Student Survey as pre-tests for the module. These two tools are intended to be used again, as post-tests, at the end of the module. A reminder has been included. Answers to the Content Quiz are shown below. The Student Survey (see page 162) is composed of subjective questions, so answers will vary. The Student Self-Evaluation Form and the Action Group Evaluation Form can also be administered at the end of the module. Finally, a Program Evaluation Form has been provided for your optional feedback.

Answers to Content Quiz

1. d. all of the above
2. b. false. The U.S. government now requires nutrition labels to help consumers be able to choose more healthful diets and regulates many terms used on labels so their meanings are standardized.
3. c.
4. a. true
5. d. Eating too much fat, particularly animal fat, increased the risk of heart disease.
6. a.
7. c. All foods supply calories, but some, such as fats and sugars, supply "empty calories."
8. a. true. Because foods high in saturated fat are often high in cholesterol, simply decreasing saturated fat in the diet helps to control dietary cholesterol as well as blood cholesterol.
9. b. Nutrients are generally classified into six groups: water, carbohydrates, proteins, fats, minerals, and vitamins.
10. a. true
11. d. all of the above
12. b. false. Salt and sodium occurs naturally in many foods, such as milk, meats, baking soda, and some vegetables.

Cross-Curricular Suggestions

Description of Activity	Curriculum Connections	When to Use
The Food Guide Pyramid is used to communicate food groups and recommended servings in a visual way. What other geometric shapes could students use to present this information? What would something like the Food Guide Hexagonal Prism look like? Have students choose a geometric shape and fill it in with the food groups and servings found in the Food Guide Pyramid. Display students' Food Guide Shapes in the classroom.	Math	Following Activity 2
Have students use pastels, chalk, watercolor, colored pencils, colored pens, or collage to create a still life that shows all of the food groups. Exhibit the art work in the school library or hallway.	Art	Following Activity 2
Have students invent a food product that is healthy for the body and for the environment and create an advertising campaign to introduce and promote it. They can create print ads, labeling, scripts for radio commercials and jingles, scripts for TV commercials, and testimonials by satisfied customers. Encourage them to study labeling on health foods to see how words such as 'natural' and 'pure' and 'organic' are used in the company names and in the labeling to appeal to consumers.	Language Arts	Following Activity 3

Description of Activity	Curriculum Connections	When to Use
Challenge students to look closely at labels in order to find "hidden" sugars in the list of ingredients. Sugar may be listed, along with smaller amounts of other forms of sugar such as fructose, sucrose, sorbital, juice concentrate, dextrose, honey, corn syrup. Students can use what they learn to create informational posters to display at a health fair or science fair.	Language Arts, Science	Following Activity 3
Water is an essential nutrient. It is found in foods, so that about one-third of the two-and-a-half quarts of water needed per day comes from eating a balanced diet. The rest comes from the tap, and 6–10 glasses of water every day are recommended for good health. Have students keep track of how much water they drink over a period of several days. Then have them average the amount to find out how many gallons of water they drink in a month.	Math	Following Activity 4
Of all the foods that people eat, chicken is served nearly worldwide. Each culture prepares chicken in a distinctive way that incorporates traditional cooking methods, native herbs and spices, regional staples such as rice and grains, and other cultural influences. Have students compile a cookbook of chicken recipes from around the world. Groups of students can focus on each continent or region, or individuals or partners may choose a particular country to investigate.	Social Studies	Following Activity 4

Explore the Issues

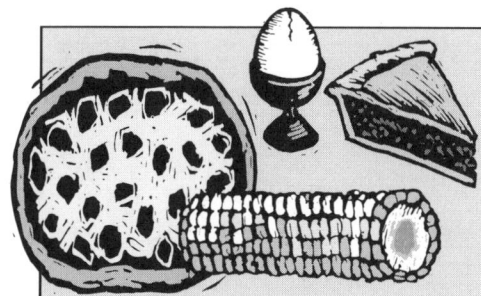

INVESTIGATE FOODS AND THE ENVIRONMENT

EXPLORE 1

Students will find out about different types of food, factors that affect food production, and ways in which food production can impact the environment.

Key Concepts

- Production of different foods requires different resources.
- Natural and human-caused factors can influence food production.
- Some methods of food production can have a negative impact on the environment.

Objectives

After completing this activity, students will be able to

- identify where different foods come from
- identify how resources are used to produce different types of foods
- identify factors that might influence food production

Prepare

Read the background information about food production in Issues and Information sections A and F.

Materials

Activity Sheet 1 for each student (See Blackline Masters section.)

Setting the Stage

Discuss briefly the questions on student page 9.

- **Where does the food you eat come from?**

  Discuss where food in stores, restaurants, and the school cafeteria comes from, including local farms and cooperatives, agricultural regions of the U.S., and overseas sources.

- **What might affect the supply of food?**

  Encourage students to consider information about food supplies worldwide. Possible answers include natural disasters such as flood, drought, pest infestation, crop failure; overgrazing and soil depletion; loss of farmland due to urbanization; lack of water and fuel or overuse of resources for production; political factors that might limit distribution; economic factors that affect distribution.

Vocabulary

➤ drought
overgrazing
soil depletion

Focus

1. Explain that production of different types of foods requires different amounts of resources. Have students study the table and discuss the questions. Have them refer to Issues and Information section A for more about food production.

- **How are grains and soybeans used to produce meats and eggs?**

  Grains and soybeans are fed to animals, which in turn are the source of meat and eggs.

Food (typical serving size)	Water Used to Produce One Serving	Grains and Soybeans Used to Produce One Serving
Lettuce (1 cup)	3 gallons	none
Tomato (1 small)	8 gallons	none
Broccoli ($\frac{1}{2}$ cup)	11 gallons	none
Whole-wheat bread—2 slices (.8 oz each slice)	15 gallons	.065 lbs
White bread—2 slices (.8 oz each slice)	21 gallons	.065 lbs
Eggs—1 egg (2.1 oz)	63 gallons	.375 lbs
Chicken with skin and bones—4 oz	165 gallons	.75 lbs
Hamburger patty—4 oz	616 gallons	4 lbs

Data derived from USDA, Economic Research Service, Beltsville, Md., as cited in Frances Moore Lappé, *Diet for a Small Planet*, Ballantine Books, 1982, p. 70 and from "Water Inputs in California Food Production," a 1991 study for the Water Education Foundation, Sacramento, CA. Water-use data include all water for raising feed, raising animals or plants, and processing; data are for food production in California only.

- **Which foods use the most water, grain, and soybean resources?**

  Beef, chicken, eggs.

- **Why does it take more water resources to make white bread than it does to make whole-wheat bread?**

  Processing of foods requires water, and white flour is more highly processed than whole-wheat flour.

- **About how many gallons of water are needed to make a sandwich using one egg, $\frac{1}{2}$ cup of lettuce, and a tomato on two slices of whole-wheat bread?**

  87.5 gallons

- **About how many gallons of water are needed to make a sandwich using a hamburger patty, $\frac{1}{2}$ cup of lettuce, and a tomato on two slices of whole-wheat bread?**

  640.5 gallons

2. Have students work in pairs to complete Activity Sheet 1.

It's a Wrap!

Review Activity Sheet 1 and discuss students' answers to It's a Wrap questions:

- **In what ways do modern food production practices impact the environment?**

	Water Used to Produce Food for One Day*	Land Used to Produce Food for One Year**
Vegan Diet	300 gallons per day	$\frac{1}{6}$ acre
Ovo-Lacto Vegetarian Diet	1200 gallons per day	$\frac{1}{2}$ acre
Meat-Based Diet	4200 gallons per day	$3\frac{1}{4}$ acres

*Estimate from *Sierra Magazine,* March/April 1995, p. 28
**Estimate from *Diet for a New America,* John Robbins, Stillpoint Publishing, 1987, p. 352

Possible answers include strain on land and water use, water pollution, soil depletion.

- **How does the typical American diet impact the environment?**

A diet that relies heavily on meat products uses more natural resources and land than a diet that relies on plant products.

You may wish to discuss the following topics in greater detail:

- It has been suggested that "eating lower on the food chain" is better for the environment and better for health. Discuss the meaning of this phrase and how eating a vegetarian diet can conserve resources.

- Display the table shown above and discuss how land and water are used to meet dietary needs and preferences.

Home

Assignment Home activity on student page 11.

People follow special diets for many different reasons. People who eat a *vegan* diet eat no animal products at all, including dairy products and eggs. People who eat an *ovo-lacto* vegetarian diet eat eggs and dairy products but no meat. In your Journal, list the ingredients for your favorite pizza with extra toppings; include ingredients used in the crust and the sauce. What ingredients would you add or take away to make a vegan pizza? What ingredients would you add or take away to make an ovo-lacto pizza?

ACTIVITY SHEET 1 EXPLORE

Name _____

FOOD PRODUCTION AND THE ENVIRONMENT (part 1)

In response to a growing world population and a growing demand in developed countries for meat, eggs, and dairy products, methods have been developed to increase food production. Although these methods do increase food production, concerns have been raised because of the environmental problems that may result.

1. Some modern food production practices are shown in the chart below, followed by a list of environmental problems. Work together with a partner to identify how environmental problems may be linked to food production practices. In each box of the chart below, write the numbers of the environmental problems (see part 2) that may arise. There may be more than one problem linked to a food production practice.

Food Production Practices

Pack foods in excessive packaging for sale in stores. **1, 2, 7**	Clear land of trees to create range land and crop land. **4, 5**	Fatten livestock by feeding them grains and soybeans grown with the help of chemical fertilizers and pesticides. **1**
Use fertilizers made from synthetic chemicals to increase crop yields. **1, 2, 4**	Raise large numbers of livestock for human consumption, which includes growing grain for feed. **1, 2, 3, 4, 5, 6**	Graze livestock on open ranges where they can eat grasses down to the roots. **5, 6**
Grow produce in large quantities in special regions, transport it to a distribution center, and then transport it to the point where it's sold. **1, 2, 7**	Use pesticides to kill pests and produce more attractive and more abundant crops. **1, 4, 6**	Grow large quantities of a single crop year after year. **6**

24 Environmental ACTION Food Teacher Resource Guide

ACTIVITY SHEET 1 EXPLORE

Name

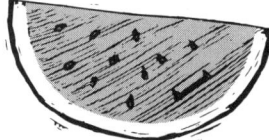

FOOD PRODUCTION AND THE ENVIRONMENT (part 2)

Environmental Problems

1. Pollution of water, air, and land
2. Use of fossil fuels (gas, oil, coal)
3. Use of fresh water
4. Destruction of natural habitats
5. Erosion of topsoil
6. Depletion of topsoil
7. Increase in waste that will need to be disposed of

2. Choose two of the food production practices and explain the possible impact they have on the environment.

Answers will vary. Students should be able to explain their reasoning for linking environmental problems with food production practices. For example, excessive packaging causes waste problems; producing the packaging uses natural resources and fossil fuels and may pollute water, air, land.

3. On a separate sheet of paper, identify some actions you, your family, your school, or your community might take to help reduce or solve the problems caused by each of the food production practices shown in the table.

Students' ideas will vary. Answers include eating a diet less dependent on animal products, eating locally grown produce, buying in bulk to avoid excessive packaging.

Explore the Issues: Investigate Foods and the Environment 25

USE THE FOOD GUIDE PYRAMID

The diet that is healthiest for people may also be healthiest for the environment. Students find out what it means to eat a healthy diet by learning about food groups and following the recommendations of the Food Guide Pyramid.

Key Concepts

- The Food Guide Pyramid recommends daily allowances for different types of foods.
- Following the Food Guide Pyramid encourages eating a healthy, balanced diet.
- Eating a balanced diet promotes good health by providing nutrients and maintaining a healthy weight level.

Objectives

After completing this activity, students will be able to
- categorize foods according to the Food Guide Pyramid
- use the Food Guide Pyramid to suggest healthy menu plans
- suggest ways to encourage healthy eating habits

Prepare

Read background material about the Food Guide Pyramid in Issues and Information section B.

Materials

- Activity Sheet 2 for each student
- measuring cups (optional)

Setting the Stage

Discuss briefly the questions on student page 13.

- **What are some reasons for choosing to eat a healthy diet?**

  Encourage students to discuss ideas that have to do with the environment as well as with personal health; help students relate diet to energy, appearance, long-term benefits, good habits.

- **What kinds of foods are in a healthy diet?**

  Answers will vary. Encourage students to take a hard look at typical eating habits.

- **What factors influence the food choices people make?**

  Encourage students to consider economics, religion, culture, family traditions, philosophical beliefs, health considerations, environmental concerns; have students suggest ways in which life style, fast foods and snack foods, and convenience foods influence choices.

Vocabulary

→ calorie
nutrient

Focus

1. The U.S. Department of Agriculture recommends some important dietary guidelines for Americans. These guidelines are illustrated by the Food Guide Pyramid. The pyramid provides an outline of what to eat each day to get the correct number of calories and nutrients while maintaining a healthy weight. As the pyramid shows, people need to eat foods from each of the five major food groups each day. Have students

study the pyramid and use it to answer the questions below.

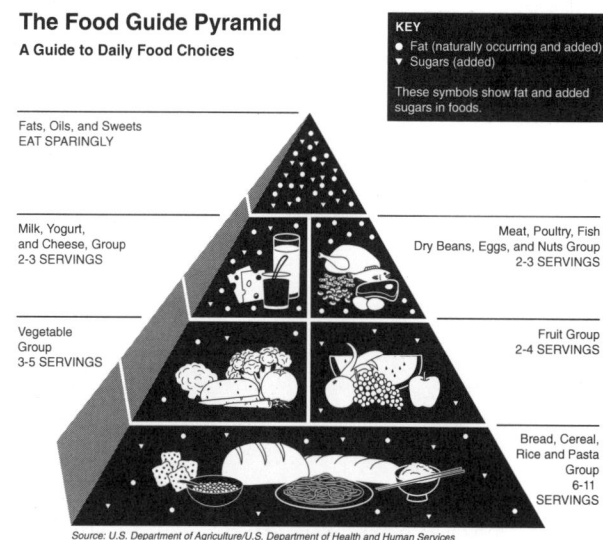

The Food Guide Pyramid
A Guide to Daily Food Choices

Source: U.S. Department of Agriculture/U.S. Department of Health and Human Services

- **How does the pyramid shape suggest a hierarchy of healthy eating?**

  Students should realize that foods that should be eaten in more limited quantities occupy the small sections at the top of the pyramid; foods that should be served throughout the day at each meal occupy the largest sections of the pyramid.

- **In what food group(s) would you put spaghetti and meat sauce?**

  bread, vegetable, meat

- **In what food group(s) would you put vegetable soup?**

  Possible answers include vegetables, meat (could be used in stock), bread (if grain such as barley is used)

- **In what food group(s) would you put a peanut butter and jelly sandwich?**

  meat (nuts), bread, fruit (may be considered a sweet, depending on ingredients)

- **Can you replace foods in one group with foods from another group? Why or why not?**

  No, for good health you need nutrients from each of the groups.

2. What the Food Guide Pyramid considers to be a serving is not necessarily the same as what one might think of as a serving or portion. The table on page 28 shows what counts as a serving. Issues and Information section B has additional information on serving size.

- **How many servings of bread are in one English muffin?**

  2

- **How many servings of which food groups do you get in a cheese sandwich?**

  2 servings of bread; 1 serving of milk

- **Think of a breakfast menu and tell how many servings of different food groups you would get.**

  Answers will vary. Encourage students to include as many food groups as they can.

3. The government has developed a 5-A-Day campaign to encourage people to increase their intake of fruits and vegetables. What ideas would you suggest to make it easier for people to get five servings a day of fruits and vegetables?

Encourage students to be creative as they brainstorm ideas. Record their responses on the chalkboard. Possible answers include drinking juice; putting lettuce and tomato on sandwiches; mixing fat-free yogurt with fruit; using fruit as a topping for pancakes, waffles, frozen yogurt, sherbet; putting vegetables on pizza or pasta or rice; keeping cut-up vegetables on hand for snacks.

4. Complete Activity Sheet 2.

It's a Wrap

Review Activity Sheet 2. Then discuss students' answers to It's a Wrap questions.

- **What are three ways to make a diet more healthy?**

  Answers will vary; encourage students to use the Food Guide Pyramid as they respond.

Food Pyramid Serving Guide

Food Group	One Serving
Bread	1 slice of bread $\frac{1}{2}$ bagel or $\frac{1}{2}$ hamburger bun 3–4 small crackers 1 oz ready-to-eat cereal $\frac{1}{2}$ cup cooked cereal, rice, or pasta
Vegetable	1 cup raw leafy vegetables $\frac{1}{2}$ cup other vegetables (cooked or raw) 1 ear corn; 1 tomato 7 or 8 baby carrots or carrot sticks 3 to 5 broccoli spears $\frac{3}{4}$ cup vegetable juice
Fruit	1 medium apple, banana, orange $\frac{1}{2}$ cup chopped, cooked or canned fruit $\frac{1}{4}$ cup dried fruit $\frac{1}{2}$ grapefruit; 15 grapes; 12 cherries $\frac{3}{4}$ cup fruit juice
Milk	1 cup milk or yogurt 2 cups cottage cheese $1\frac{1}{2}$ oz natural cheese 2 oz processed cheese
Meat	2–3 oz cooked lean meat, poultry, or fish (1 medium skinless chicken breast or 2 skinless drumsticks) 1 to $1\frac{1}{2}$ cups cooked dry beans 2–3 eggs $\frac{2}{3}$ to 1 cup nuts 4–6 Tbs peanut butter

- **Name some ways in which healthy eating can contribute to a healthy environment.**

  Possible answers include eating fewer animal products, eating fresh fruits and vegetables that are local and/or organic to cut down on use of energy and pesticides; eating whole grains and other less-processed foods to cut down on use of energy and chemicals.

  You may wish to have students explore the following topics in more detail.

- Demonstrate what a serving size is by bringing in measuring cups, measuring spoons, some glasses, a food scale, and a variety of foods (rice, can of tuna, lettuce, soup, mashed potatoes). Or put the following information on the chalkboard and discuss it to further students' understanding :
  - $\frac{1}{2}$ cup is the size of a small fist
  - 1 cup is the size of a small hand holding a tennis ball
  - 3 ounces of meat, fish, or poultry is about the size of a deck of cards

- Studies by the U.S.D.A. Food and Nutrition Service in the early 90s found that 35% of elementary school children and almost 60% of teenagers do not eat fruit, and about 35% of school-age children do not eat any vegetables. Also, the selection of vegetables lacks variety—for example, they always choose potatoes that are fried. Discuss how these findings differ from the recommendations of the Food Guide Pyramid.

- Discuss the relationship between the typical American diet and diseases that are prevalent in, if not unique to Western culture, such as heart disease and certain forms of cancer. The typical American meat-based diet has about 40% of calories from fat; the dietary guidelines recommend less than 30%. The typical American diet contains twice as much protein as needed according to the guidelines, too much salt, too much sugar, and too little fiber. Americans are becoming much more aware of this link and are changing their diets accordingly.

Home

Follow-Up Have students compare how their favorite pizzas changed according to each dietary plan.

Assignment Home activity on student page 16.

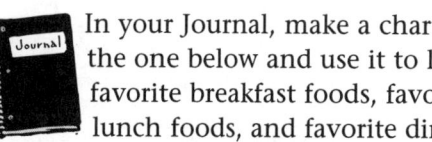

In your Journal, make a chart like the one below and use it to list your favorite breakfast foods, favorite lunch foods, and favorite dinner foods. Then assign each food on your list to a food group on the Food Guide Pyramid. Estimate how many servings there are on your list in each group. Add up the servings in each food group. How did your list compare to the recommended servings for one day?

Food Item	Food Group	Servings

Explore the Issues: Use the Food Guide Pyramid 29

ACTIVITY SHEET

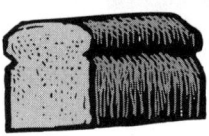

Name

THE FOOD GUIDE PYRAMID (part 1)

Complete the drawing of the Food Guide Pyramid, including the names of the basic foods in each of the food groups. In part 2, fill in the recommended servings per day according to your needs as shown in the chart below. You may want to draw pictures of some of the food items in each group.

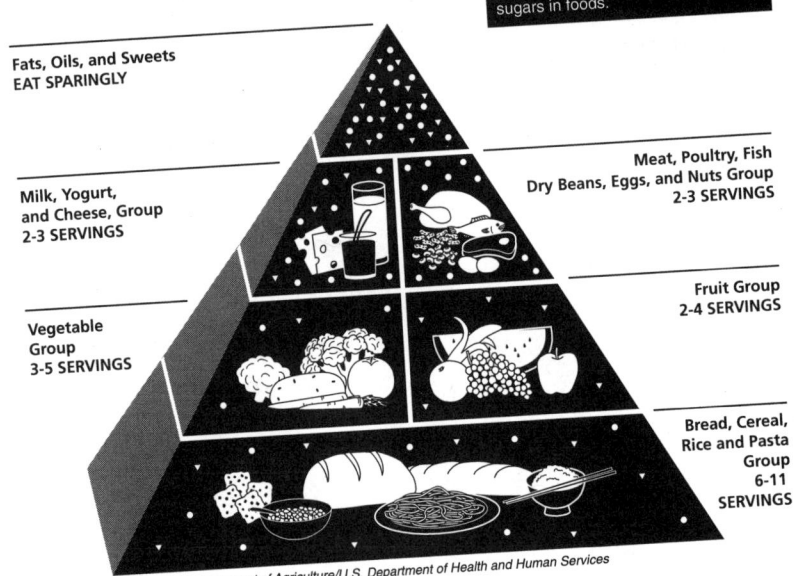

Recommended Daily Servings

Food Group	For Teenage Boys*	For Teenage Girls**	For All Ages
Bread	11	9	6–11
Vegetable	5	4	3–5
Fruit	4	3	2–4
Milk	3	3	2–3
Meat	2–3 (or 7 ounces)	2 (or 6 ounces)	2–3
Fats, sweets	Use sparingly	Use sparingly	Use sparingly

* and for active men and very active women   ** and for most children, active women, and sedentary men

30 Environmental ACTION Food   Teacher Resource Guide

ACTIVITY SHEET

Name _____

THE FOOD GUIDE PYRAMID (part 2)

Create a menu plan for one day that includes breakfast, lunch, dinner, and snacks and meets the requirements of the Food Guide Pyramid. Remember that fats, oils, and sweets are to be used only sparingly. Use the chart below to create your menu and tally the servings for each food group.

Meal	Food Group	Number of Servings
BREAKFAST		
LUNCH		
DINNER		
SNACKS		

Explore the Issues: Use the Food Guide Pyramid 31

EVALUATE NUTRITIONAL VALUES

People need to get certain nutrients from their diets in order to be healthy. Americans tend to get too little of some nutrients and too much of some others. Students will learn about nutrients and the guidelines for maintaining good health through a well-balanced diet.

Key Concepts

- The energy stored in food is measured in calories.
- Foods contain nutrients, the sources of nourishment that are needed for healthy growth.
- Some foods contain added fats, sugars, and salts that should be avoided.

Objectives

After completing this activity, students will be able to
- identify foods that contain added fats, sugars, and salts
- compare foods to make healthy choices
- read and interpret food labels

Prepare

Read about calories, nutrients, food additives, and labeling in Issues and Information sections C and D.

Materials

Activity Sheet 3 for each student

Setting the Stage

Discuss briefly the questions on student page 18.

- **What are nutrients?**

  sources of nourishment; the components in food that provide energy and building materials for the body's metabolism

- **What are some nutrients that are essential for a healthy diet?**

  Essentials are water, carbohydrates, some fats, proteins, various minerals and vitamins.

- **How can you identify the nutrients in different foods?**

  Read food labels; consult a reference book, pamphlet, or food composition database.

Vocabulary

 carbohydrate
cholesterol
metabolism
minerals
proteins
saturated fat
sodium
sugar
vitamins

Focus

1. Have students read Issues and Information sections C and D and study the following list of USDA Dietary Guidelines:

- Eat a variety of foods.
- Maintain a healthy weight.
- Choose a diet low in fat, saturated fat, and cholesterol.
- Choose a diet with plenty of vegetables, fruits, and grain products.
- Use sugars only in moderation.
- Use salt and sodium only in moderation.
- Children and adolescents should not drink alcoholic beverages.

2. Have students provide examples of foods that contain fats, saturated fats, cholesterol, and sodium, and list their responses on the chalkboard. Ask where these foods are located in the Food Guide Pyramid. Answers will include deep-fried, salty, and high-fat snack foods, such as French fries, potato chips, cookies. Students will note that these foods all belong in the smallest section of the Food Guide Pyramid and should be eaten only sparingly.

3. Have students look at the chart below for information about fat and sugar and then answer the questions.

- **What are calories?**

   In nutrition, calories are the units by which the energy contained in foods is measured.

- **What are some examples of foods with high amounts of added sugars?**

   Possible answers include soft drinks, candies, some low-fat yogurts, low-fat cookies, cakes and pies, some canned fruits, jams and jellies.

- **Why might a person need more or fewer calories than these averages?**

   More calories are needed for very active people, such as athletes, and for pregnant women; fewer calories are needed for less active people.

- **The chart below shows how much fat and sugar is within healthy limits in our diets, but how can you find out how much you're getting in different foods?**

   Read food labels; consult a reference book, pamphlet, or food composition database.

4. Have students complete the work on Activity Sheet 3.

It's a Wrap

Students make a poster or radio or TV announcement promoting either the increased or decreased consumption of a particular nutrient. They should include information about which foods to eat or to avoid and why.

Home

Follow-Up Discuss students' menus. Which meals do students need to focus on to maintain a healthy diet?

Assignment Home activity on student page 19.

Read at least one food label from a can, package, or box. Copy the label in your Journal and write a few sentences telling why you think this food would or would not be a good addition to a healthy diet.

Recommended Daily Number of Calories and Limits of Fat and Added Sugar

	For Teenage Boys	For Teenage Girls	For All Ages
Total Calories	2800	2200	1600–2800
Total Fat * (grams)	93	73	53–93
Total Added Sugar * (teaspoons)	18	12	6–18

* Refer to Issues and Information section E for more information about fats and added sugars.
Note: 1 tsp. sugar = 4 grams; 1 tsp. fat = 4 grams

Explore the Issues: Evaluate Nutritional Values

Name _____

ACTIVITY SHEET 3 EXPLORE

FOOD LABELS (part 1)

Compare the three food labels shown below and use them to answer the questions.

Nutrition Facts	Wheat Squares Sweetened		Corn Flakes Not Sweetened		Mixed Grain Flakes Sweetened	
Serving Size 1 Box	(35g)		(19g)		(27g)	
Serving per container	1		1		1	
Amount Per Serving						
Calories 90	120		70		100	
Calories from fat	0		0		0	
	% Daily Value*		% Daily Value*		% Daily Value*	
Total Fat	0g	0%	0g	0%	0g	0%
Saturated Fat	0g	0%	0g	0%	0g	0%
Cholesterol	0mg	0%	0mg	0%	0mg	0%
Sodium	0mg	0%	200mg	8%	120mg	5%
Potassium	125mg	4%	25mg	1%	30mg	1%
Total Carbohydrate	29g	10%	17g	6%	24g	8%
Dietary Fiber	3g	12%	1g	4%	1g	4%
Sugars	5g		6g		13g	
Protein	4g		1g		1g	
Vitamin A				10%		10%
Vitamin C		0%		15%		90%
Calcium		0%		0%		0%
Iron		0%		6%		20%
Thiamin		10%		15%		20%
Riboflavin		30%		15%		20%
Niacin		30%		15%		20%
Vitamin B_6		30%		15%		20%

* Percent Daily Values are based on a 2,000-calorie diet. Your daily values may be higher or lower depending on your calorie needs:

	Calories	2,000	2,500
Total Fat	Less than	65g	80g
Sat Fat	Less than	20g	25g
Cholesterol	Less than	300mg	300mg
Sodium	Less than	2,400mg	2,400mg
Potassium	Less than	3,500mg	3,500mg
Total Carbohydrate		300g	375g
Dietary Fiber		25g	30g

Source: Food and Drug Administration

ACTIVITY SHEET

Name

FOOD LABELS (part 2)

1. Which nutrients do the labels indicate are included in these cereals?
   Answers include sodium, potassium, carbohydrates (including fiber and sugars), protein, some vitamins and minerals

2. Which of these cereals would you choose if you were on a low-salt diet?
   wheat squares

3. Which would you avoid if you were on a low-salt diet?
   corn flakes

4. Which of these cereals would you choose if you wanted to lose weight, and why would you choose it?
   unsweetened corn flakes—lowest in calories and in sugars and fats

5. What other information do you get from these labels to help you compare these cereals?
   Answers include amounts of different vitamins, calcium, iron, and amino acids; percent of daily values for different nutrients that you get from each cereal; a table that is a guide to how much you should get of different nutrients each day, and so on. Point out that labels also list the ingredients in a product from largest amount to smallest amount; a cereal with sugar listed as the second ingredient or different tyes of sugar listed in the various ingredients may not be the best choice.

PRACTICE MAKING FOOD CHOICES

Making healthy food choices means understanding how food is used by the body to maintain good health. Students will find out more about essential nutrients and the foods that provide them.

Key Concepts

- Some foods have important health benefits.
- Appropriate amounts of essential nutrients are necessary for good health.
- Different foods provide specific nutrients.

Objectives

After completing this activity, students will be able to

- identify essential nutrients
- identify effects of not getting proper nutrition from diet
- identify healthy food choices for good nutrition and for the environment

Prepare

Read background material on essential nutrients in Issues and Information sections C, E, and F.

Materials

- Activity Sheet 4 for each student
- cookbooks (optional)

Setting the Stage

Discuss briefly the questions on student page 21.

- **How can the Food Guide Pyramid help you make healthy food choices?**

   Remind students that fruits, vegetables, and grains—foods closer to the base of the pyramid—should be eaten in the greatest quantity; foods close to the top of the pyramid—fats, sugars, high-sodium foods—should be eaten only in very small quantities.

- **How do healthy food choices help the environment?**

   Remind students that products derived from animals—meat, dairy, eggs—take more land and more water to produce than fruits, vegetables, and grains; choosing foods that are not highly processed, are grown locally, or are available in bulk quantities that do not require elaborate packaging are also easier on the environment in terms of natural energy resources and air and water pollution.

Vocabulary

➤ amino acid
fortified
glucose
starch

Focus

1. The chart below summarizes how essential nutrients are used in the body. Have students study the chart and then answer the questions. You may also wish to have students review the background material in Issues and Information sections C, E, and F.

Some Essential Nutrients

Nutrients	Foods that Supply Them	How They Are Used in the Body

Carbohydrates:
  starch
 	
  sugars
	bread, crackers, noodles, cereal, grain, peas, potatoes, beans
	honey, syrup, fruit, table sugar
		provide energy; starch is a chain of simple sugars linked together; when starches and sugars break down, energy is released

Fats	oils, butter, margarine, whole milk, cheese, eggs, meat, poultry, nuts, olives	provide energy; provide building materials for the body; provide insulation; fats can be stored and may be used later
Proteins	beef, pork, poultry, fish, eggs, milk, nuts	provide amino acids needed for cell growth and repair; a protein is a chain of amino acids linked together—20 different kinds of amino acids link together in different combinations to produce proteins; 12 amino acids can be made by the body, but the other 8 must come from food

Vitamins
  A
 	
  B complex
 	
  C
 	
  D
 	
  E
  K
	
	green and yellow vegetables, fruit, egg yolks, liver, milk, butter
	meat, milk, liver, eggs, grains
	
	citrus fruit, tomatoes, potatoes, green leafy vegetables, alfalfa sprouts
	fortified milk, eggs, liver, tuna; made by skin in sunlight
	vegetable oils, milk, grains
	green leafy vegetables, tomatoes, grains
		
		healthy eyes, hair, skin
		
		releases energy from glucose; help heart and nerves function; healthy skin
		healthy bones, teeth, gums; resistance to infection
		
		healthy bones and teeth
		
		healthy cells
		blood clotting; liver function

Minerals
  calcium
 	
  phosphorous
 	
  potassium
  sodium
  magnesium
 	
  iron
 	
  iodine
  zinc
	
	dairy products, fish, eggs, green leafy vegetables
	dairy products, beans, meat, whole grains, nuts, broccoli
	bananas, fruits, meat, vegetables, milk
	table salt, most foods
	green leafy vegetables, milk, meat, potatoes, grains
	liver, red meat, egg yolks, nuts, beans, green leafy vegetables
	fish, shellfish, iodized table salt
	meat, eggs, dried beans and peas, milk, green vegetables, eggs, seafood
		
		strong bones, teeth, muscles; blood clotting; nerve function
		bones, teeth, nerve and muscle function
		
		nerve and muscle function
		nerve function; amount of water in body
		nerve and muscle function; making proteins
		oxygen in red blood cells
		
		controls rate at which food is used
		healing wounds; making proteins

Water	most foods	needed for chemical changes and most body functions; needed in greatest quantity

- **What should you eat if you have a broken arm?**

  Answers include citrus fruits, tomatoes, potatoes, green leafy vegetables, fortified milk and other dairy products, eggs, beans, broccoli, seafood, meat or other protein.

- **What should you eat to help you have healthy teeth?**

  Answers include dairy products, fish, eggs, green, leafy vegetables, beans, meat, grains, nuts, broccoli, citrus fruits, tomatoes, tuna.

- **What mineral is found in most foods?**

  sodium

- **What could you eat for breakfast to keep your skin and hair healthy?**

  Suggested responses include fruit, eggs, buttered toast, oatmeal.

- **Why is water an important nutrient?**

  Water is a key factor in chemical changes and body functions.

2. Have students work in small groups to complete Activity Sheet 4.

Students may refer to the chart in the lesson, the Food Guide Pyramid, and the material in Issues and Information as they work.

It's a Wrap

Discuss each group's work on Activity Sheet 4. How do students' menus compare to the menus they created using the Food Guide Pyramid alone? Compare menus for Activity Sheet 3 and Activity Sheet 4. Then discuss students ideas about It's a Wrap questions.

- **Why are food choices important for health and for the environment?**

  Foods can be chosen that provide certain essential nutrients that the body needs in order to function; some food choices are healthier for the environment, too, in terms of how land, energy resources, and water are used.

- **What are three food choices that will make your diet healthier?**

  Answers will vary. Discuss which foods students do not eat very often and strategies for increasing them in the diet.

  You may wish to have students discuss the following topics in further detail.

- Encourage discussion about the fact that food choice is very personal, can be very emotional, and can be as hard to change as any habit; there can be economic considerations; radical changes in diet (diet fads, for example) can result in not getting enough nutrients and consequent health problems.

- Have students think of ways that consumer demand has changed what foods are available. For example, the development of more processed foods and convenience foods; more health-conscious foods, such as reduced-salt, reduced-fat, reduced-cholesterol items; the development of fat and sugar substitutes.

Home

Follow-Up Have students compare the labels they chose. What surprised them most about the ingredients?

Assignment Home activity on student page 23.

Interview the manager of a supermarket, health food store, restaurant, fast food restaurant, or other food-related business in your community and see what information is available either about the nutritional contents of the products that are sold or what is done to promote good nutrition. Is the person familiar with the "5-A-Day for Better Health" fruits and vegetables campaign? Make a report in your Journal of what you found.

ACTIVITY SHEET 4
EXPLORE

Name _____

CHOOSING FOODS (part 1)

Use the following list of foods to create healthy and well-balanced breakfast, lunch, and dinner menus for at least three days. Use classroom resources, the Food Guide Pyramid, the nutrient chart, and Issues and Information as you work together in small groups.

- apple
- bagel and cream cheese
- baked beans
- banana
- beef stew
- bran muffin
- bread
- carrots
- cereal (corn flakes, raisin bran)
- cheese
- cheese omelet
- chicken
- chicken noodle soup
- cole slaw
- egg salad
- fruit salad
- green salad
- hamburger
- lentil soup
- macaroni salad
- meatballs
- milk
- noodles
- oatmeal
- orange
- orange juice
- pancakes
- pasta
- peanut butter and jelly
- pear
- pork
- potatoes
- potato salad
- power shake (yogurt, fruit, juice)
- rice
- stir-fry vegetables
- tacos
- tomatoes
- tomato soup
- tuna sandwich
- turkey club sandwich
- water
- yogurt

DAY 1

BREAKFAST
_____
_____
_____
_____
_____

LUNCH
_____
_____
_____
_____
_____

DINNER
_____
_____
_____
_____
_____

DAY 2

BREAKFAST
_____
_____
_____
_____
_____

LUNCH
_____
_____
_____
_____
_____

LUNCH
_____
_____
_____
_____
_____

Explore the Issues: Practice Making Food Choices 39

ACTIVITY SHEET 4 EXPLORE

Name

CHOOSING FOODS (part 2)

DAY 3

BREAKFAST	LUNCH	DINNER

1. How does using the nutrient chart influence your choices? What other considerations are there?

   Answers will vary but should indicate how the Food Guide Pyramid and nutrient chart were used, as well as taste preferences, combinations, cost, and so on.

2. How does food preparation relate to nutrition?

   How food is prepared can influence fat and nutrient content. For example, roasted chicken is healthier than fried chicken; raw or steamed vegetables retain more nutrients than vegetables cooked for a long time.

3. What foods would you add to the menus that are not on the list?

   Answers will vary.

40 Environmental ACTION Food Teacher Resource Guide

Analyze

LEARN FROM ROLE MODELS IN THE COMMUNITY

Students learn about diet and nutrition issues from a community resource person.

Objectives

After completing this activity, students will be able to
- identify features of a balanced diet
- give examples of health programs in the community that provide nutrition education
- describe ways in which eating habits and nutrition can be improved

Prepare

Make arrangements for a resource person from your community to address the class about nutrition issues. Possible speakers include dieticians, local organic growers, cooks, community food bank volunteers, health food store employees, university extension volunteers, grocers.

Activity Sheet 5 may be used as a guide in preparing the presentation. You may also provide a list of the students' questions in advance.

It is not expected that the speaker will be an expert in all areas outlined on Activity Sheet 5. It is important, however, that students understand how the information in the presentation relates to the overall scope of inquiry in this activity. For areas in which the speaker does not have expertise, it would be helpful to suggest where students can go to find needed information.

Materials

Activity Sheet 5 for each student (See Blackline Masters section.)

Setting the Stage

Discuss briefly the questions on student page 27.

- **What is a balanced diet?**

   Remind students of what they have learned about the Food Guide Pyramid and important nutrients that come from eating a healthy and varied diet.

- **How are nutrition and health issues addressed in the community?**

   Responses include any known ways in which the community fosters support of nutrition and health issues, for example, through community awareness programs or community-sponsored events such as walk-a-thons and fairs.

- **How can people in the community help to improve the eating habits and health of the citizens?**

   Responses include ideas for health education, community-sponsored health projects, and increased nutrition awareness.

Focus

1. Before the speaker comes to class, explain that students will be finding out about nutrition issues in the community.

2. The speaker will discuss nutrition and health. Students will find out how the resource person functions within the community and ways in which nutrition and health are linked to the environment. Encourage students to use Activity Sheet 5 to take notes during the presentation.

Have students identify main points for each topic outlined on Activity Sheet 5 and areas that need more investigation.

Have volunteers share their ideas about how the presentation helped them find out more about nutrition and health in the community.

It's a Wrap

Have students identify main points for each topic outlined on Activity Sheet 5 and areas that need more investigation.

Have volunteers share their ideas about how the presentation helped them find out more about nutrition and health in the community.

Home

Follow-Up Discuss what students found out during their interviews. Point out that some supermarkets have a nutritional chart about the 5-a-Day campaign on the plastic bags for produce; many fast food places have nutritional charts as hand-outs or on posters on the wall; some restaurants code menu items according to their health for your heart. How does what they learned correspond to what they found out from the guest speaker?

Assignment Home activity on student page 28.

Choose a favorite after-school, study, ballgame, or movie snack. What do you like to munch? Analyze your snack choice according to four criteria: the Food Guide Pyramid (see student page 14), the nutrient chart (see student pages 22–23), the food chain, and your own personal preference. Why are treats that taste good often unhealthy choices?

ACTIVITY SHEET

Name _____

 # NOTES ON NUTRITION, DIET, AND HEALTH (part 1)

Use this sheet to record information you learn from the guest speakers who talk to you about nutrition, diet, and health issues.

Resource Person's Name _____

Title _____

Information about Diet and Nutrients

Nutrition and Health
_____
_____
_____
_____
_____

Health in the Community
_____
_____
_____
_____

Information about Food Production

Foods Produced Locally
_____
_____
_____
_____

Foods Brought in from Outside the Region
_____
_____
_____
_____

Analyze: Learn from Role Models in the Community

ACTIVITY SHEET

Name

NOTES ON NUTRITION, DIET, AND HEALTH (part 2)

Transportation Issues

Ideas for Further Investigation

Questions

TOUR THE SCHOOL CAMPUS

Students learn about diet and nutrition issues related to food service on the school campus from a resource person. They tour the campus and list information about food sources and preparation, cost, and nutrition considerations.

Objectives

After completing this activity, students will be able to
- describe how food is provided on the school campus
- list features of food preparation on the school campus
- identify where food on the school campus comes from

Prepare

Arrange for a school employee from the cafeteria or food service staff to address the class about how food decisions are made on campus and who makes them.

Activity Sheet 6 may be used as a guide in preparing the presentation. You may also provide a list of the students' questions in advance. The staff resource person should be familiar enough with the school campus to take students on a tour and answer questions.

Materials

Activity Sheet 6 for each student

Setting the Stage

Discuss briefly the questions on student page 30.

- **What kinds of foods are available on the school campus?**

  Students should describe what they know about breakfast and lunch service, snacks provided in classrooms and/or in vending machines, and how and where meals are served.

- **How are campus food decisions made?**

  Students should pinpoint how nutrition, preference, cost, and other factors might influence decisions about what is served. Students may also explore district or state policies regarding food service in schools.

Focus

1. Have students think of questions that they want to ask the resource person and record them in their Journals. The following topics can be used as guidelines:

- what food guidelines are issued by the government, state, or district
- how menus are developed
- how food is budgeted and what happens to leftovers
- what outside vendors provide entrees, packaged items for vending machines, or other prepared foods

2. Students will tour the campus and find out about the main food service features. Activity Sheet 6 can be used for taking notes and pinpointing food service locations. Details can be added when students return to class.

Analyze: Tour the School Campus **47**

It's a Wrap

Have students discuss their work on Activity Sheet 6, identifying factors to consider when analyzing food service on campus. Also provide opportunities for students to find answers to any questions they still have. Then have volunteers share how the tour helped them find out more about food service on campus.

Home

Follow-Up Have students share their analysis of favorite treats.

Assignment Home activity on student page 31.

 Sometimes you just have to use "mind over matter" to talk yourself into eating foods that are good for you. Think of a healthy after-school snack. Write a description in your Journal that will give it mouth-watering appeal.

Name _____

ACTIVITY SHEET

CAMPUS FOOD SERVICE FEATURES (part 1)

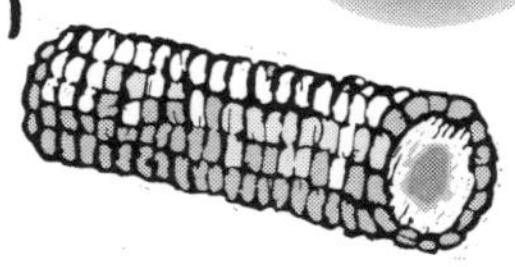

Fill in the chart below with information about where food is served on campus and where it comes from. Include information about cost and any nutrition notes you can add as you tour the campus.

Plan for Campus Food Service Audit

Location	Food	Source (vendors; ingredients for on-site preparation)	Cost and Packaging	Nutrition Notes

Analyze: Tour the School Campus   49

ACTIVITY SHEET

CAMPUS FOOD SERVICE FEATURES (part 2)

Plan for Campus Food Service Audit

Name

Location	Food	Source (vendors; ingredients for on-site preparation)	Cost and Packaging	Nutrition Notes

50   Environmental ACTION   Food   Teacher Resource Guide

PREPARE YOUR AUDIT

Using the information collected on Activity Sheet 6 and the campus tour notes, students will divide the campus into study areas for the audit.

Objectives

After completing this activity, students will be able to
- identify where food is prepared, served, or sold on campus
- identify what kinds of foods are served on campus and how they are packaged

Materials

Activity Sheet 7 for each student

Setting the Stage

Discuss briefly the questions on student page 33.

- **What are the main areas where food is prepared or served on the school campus?**

  Encourage students to think of all the food choices they can make during the school day.

- **What foods are available at each place?**

  Encourage students to identify the different types of foods and how they are served or packaged.

- **How will you audit the campus food service?**

  Encourage students to share ideas about what they want to find out about how foods are prepared, where they come from, outside vendors that provide food for the cafeteria or for machines, and criteria for menu decisions.

Focus

1. Have the class use activity sheets and notes to plan a strategy for auditing campus food service.

2. Encourage students to share their ideas about how the campus can be divided up to determine the audit sites they will study.

3. Divide the class into Action Groups and assign a study area to each one. Then have the groups meet to organize their audit. Students will record their decisions on Activity Sheet 7.

It's a Wrap

Encourage students to share their ideas about how the food service areas can effectively be audited so that important factors are not overlooked. Remind students to take into consideration environmental factors as well as health factors as they gather information.

Analyze: Prepare Your Audit   **51**

Home

Follow-Up Have students share their appetizing snack food descriptions.

Assignment Home activity on student page 34.

 Describe your favorite dish at your favorite restaurant. Where does it fit in the Food Guide Pyramid? Are other choices on the menu better in terms of health and nutrition?

ACTIVITY SHEET

Name _____

Action Group _____

CAMPUS AUDIT PLAN (part 1)

Complete the following chart to record your plan for auditing campus food service sites.

Plan for Campus Food Service Audit

Study Area/ Types of Food	Notes about Food Preparation, Vendors, Packaging	Action Group (Student Names)	Permission Required/ Accessibility	Audit Due Date

Analyze: Prepare Your Audit   53

ACTIVITY SHEET — ANALYZE

Name _____

Action Group _____

CAMPUS AUDIT PLAN (part 2)

Plan for Campus Food Service Audit

Study Area/ Types of Food	Notes about Food Preparation, Vendors, Packaging	Action Group (Student Names)	Permission Required/ Accessibility	Audit Due Date

54   Environmental ACTION   Food   Teacher Resource Guide

CONDUCT YOUR AUDIT

Action Groups will investigate their study areas and use their observations to list features related to source, preparation, nutrition, cost.

Objectives

After completing the activity, students will be able to
- describe the foods served in their study area
- list sources for foods served in their study area

Materials
- Activity Sheet 8 for each student

Setting the Stage

Discuss briefly the questions on student page 36.

- **What foods are served in your group's study area?**

    Students should be able to identify the foods that are served, including side dishes, drinks, desserts.

- **What factors influence the foods that are served?**

    Students should identify positive and negative factors that might affect the food choices. For example, is the food refrigerated? Is it prepackaged for a vending machine? Is it served hot? Is it prepared on campus or provided by an outside vendor?

Focus

1. Students working in their Action Groups can evaluate their study area and then use their observations to evaluate the site.

2. Students can investigate the types of foods served at their site in order to become more familiar with how food service decisions are made and how choices can be enhanced.

3. Have students in Action Groups work together to complete Activity Sheet 8, outlining their strategies for completing the audit.

It's a Wrap

Have students in their Action Groups review Activity Sheet 8 and the evaluations they made. Have them think of three things they discovered about their study area and three things they need to find out.

Home

Follow-Up Have students share their favorite restaurant meals. What could they do to make their choices more nutritious? How could they use the Food Guide Pyramid to make healthier choices?

Assignment Home activity on student page 36.

 Create a menu for your birthday dinner, featuring all of your favorite foods. Write a note beside each item to tell what nutrients it provides (see student pages 22–23) or where it fits into the Food Guide Pyramid (student page 14).

ACTIVITY SHEET

Action Group _____

Name _____

DETAILS OF STUDY AREA (part 1)

Look at the foods served in your study area.
Record details of your observations in the chart below.
Then, in part 2, assign food choices to sections of the Food Guide Pyramid.

Food Choices	How Foods Are Prepared	Ingredients	Food and/or Packaging Waste

Analyze: Conduct Your Audit 57

ACTIVITY SHEET

Action Group

Name _____

DETALS OF STUDY AREA (part 2)

The Food Guide Pyramid
A Guide to Daily Food Choices

KEY
● Fat (naturally occurring and added)
▼ Sugars (added)

These symbols show fat and added sugars in foods.

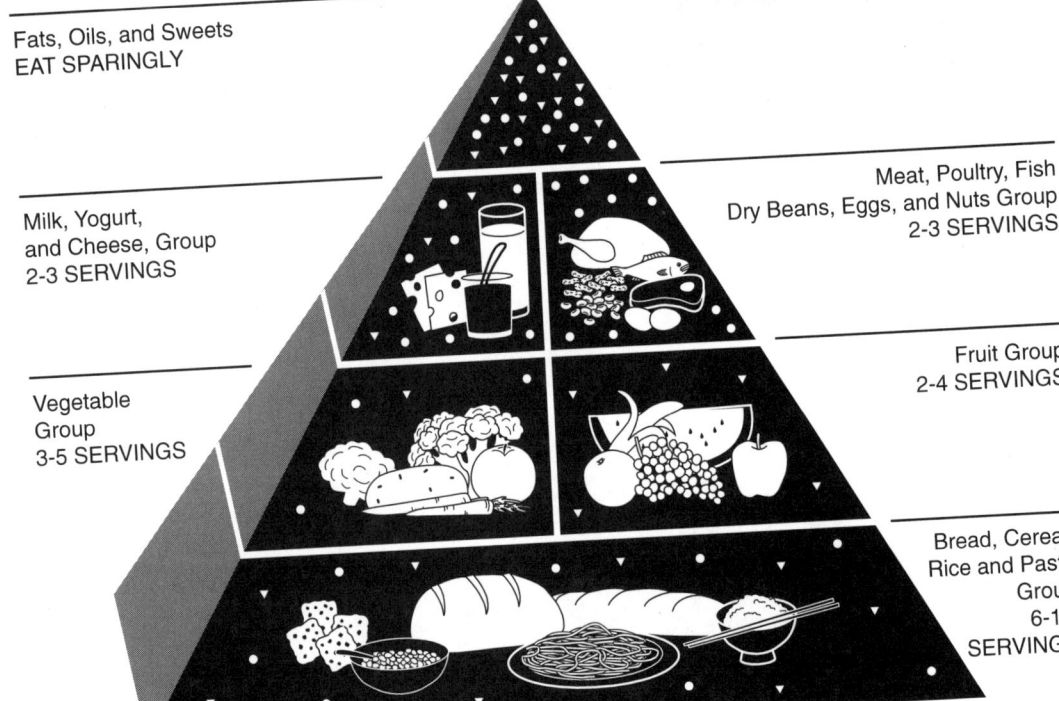

Fats, Oils, and Sweets
EAT SPARINGLY

Milk, Yogurt, and Cheese, Group
2-3 SERVINGS

Meat, Poultry, Fish
Dry Beans, Eggs, and Nuts Group
2-3 SERVINGS

Vegetable Group
3-5 SERVINGS

Fruit Group
2-4 SERVINGS

Bread, Cereal, Rice and Pasta Group
6-11 SERVINGS

Source: U.S. Department of Agriculture/U.S. Department of Health and Human Services

RESEARCH INGREDIENTS IN FOOD CHOICES

Students will research what goes into the foods that are served and identify the nutrients they provide.

Objectives

After completing this activity, students will be able to

- identify the ingredients in the foods that are served at their study areas
- identify the nutrients that each food provides

Materials

Activity Sheet 9

Setting the Stage

Discuss briefly the questions on student page 38.

- **In researching foods served in your study area, what kinds of information will be useful to you?**

  Responses include serving sizes, food choices, ingredients.

- **How will you find the information you need?**

  Responses include asking school food service workers, looking in cookbooks, calling local dieticians or university extension services.

Focus

Students will use Activity Sheet 9 as a guideline for finding out about the nutrients found in the foods that are served in their study area.

It's a Wrap

Invite groups to share their findings, as well as strategies for finding information. Can students make some generalizations about healthy food choices? Are some foods more popular than others? Based on what they have learned, should certain foods be eliminated and others increased?

Home

Follow-Up Encourage students to share the nutritional values of their favorite meals. How can the food choices or preparation be changed to offer a healthier, more balanced meal?

Assignment Home activity on student page 38.

 Using the Food Guide Pyramid (student page 14) and nutrient chart (student pages 22-23) as a guide, create a main dish that is both healthy and tasty. You may wish to create a big salad, a taco platter, or a pasta dish. Name your creation and write up the recipe.

Analyze: Research Ingredients in Food Choices

ACTIVITY SHEET 9 ANALYZE

Name _____

FOOD DATA SHEET

Use the following chart to collect information about the foods served in your assigned area.

FOOD CHOICES	NUTRIENTS

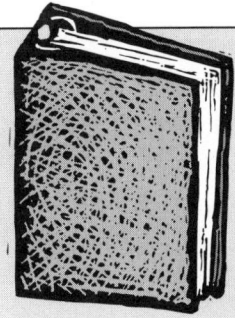

SUMMARIZE FINDINGS

Students will review audit results, evaluate the types of foods that are served, describe their nutritional value, and summarize their findings.

Objectives

After completing this activity, students will be able to
- describe foods served in their study areas
- describe how healthy choices can be offered in their study areas

Materials

Activity Sheet 10

Setting the Stage

Discuss briefly the questions on student page 40.

- **What foods are served in your study area?**

  Responses should include main dishes, side dishes, desserts, drinks, snacks.

- **What nutrients do the foods at your study area provide?**

  Responses should describe the nutritional value of the ingredients in the foods served.

- **What problems are associated with the choices at your study area?**

  Students should describe specific problems, such as high fat or sugar content, not enough variety, waste because of serving size or taste, excessive packaging, and similar observations.

Focus

1. Meet as a group to compile findings from all of the Action Groups. Each group will give a report about its observations, including the following points:
- assessing the nutritional value of the food choices in your group's study area
- offering more foods that encourage healthy choices
- identifying problems such as wasted food, excessive packaging, low nutritional value
- making any other observations about how food choices are affected at the site

Students will record information from the class discussion on Activity Sheet 10.

2. Students will meet in their Action Groups to discuss and compare healthy and unhealthy food choices at their sites. One member of the group should take notes, listing the pros and cons in two columns. For example, on the plus side, apples might be offered in the vending machines. On the other hand, processed, sugar-added applesauce in plastic packaging may be offered as a side dish.

3. When discussions are completed, group members should work together to write a one-page summary of conclusions that were reached and present the summary to the class.

It's a Wrap

Discuss campus food service practices, pinpointing how the food service can be improved to encourage better nutrition, greater variety, more environmentally friendly packaging and disposal. Then have each student write a paragraph telling how his or her group's summary addressed those topics.

Home

Follow-Up Have students share their recipes.

Assignment Home activity on student page 41.

Look through your kitchen and list the different types of sacks, boxes, and wrappers used to package foods. Which of these items can be recycled? Which can be reused? How much food packaging does your family toss out in a day?

ACTIVITY SHEET

CAMPUS FOOD SERVICE (part 1)

Name

Action Group

Combine the audit results from all Action Groups on the chart below.

Foods Served at All Study Areas

Food Choices	Nutritional Value	Waste (Packaging and Uneaten Food)	Notes

Analyze: Summarize Findings   63

ACTIVITY SHEET

Name
Action Group

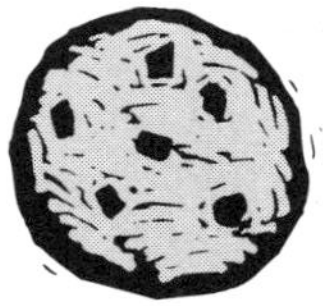

CAMPUS FOOD SERVICE (part 2)

Foods Served at All Study Areas

Food Choices	Nutritional Value	Waste (Packaging and Uneaten Food)	Notes

64 Environmental ACTION Food Teacher Resource Guide

ACT LOCALLY

Students can use the following outreach activities to apply their learning, share information, and strengthen their ties to the community.

1. Write an article for the school paper about making healthy, balanced food choices in the cafeteria.

2. Volunteer at a community food bank to find out how balanced, nutritious meals are provided at little or no charge.

3. Create a series of posters to display in the cafeteria to persuade students to make food choices that are healthy for the body and the environment.

Consider Options

EVALUATE FOOD CHOICES

Students will now begin looking at specific ways to improve the food choices they make. They will first review the reports completed during Activity 10 and then evaluate the food choices at each study area.

Objectives

After completing this activity, students will be able to

- explain how knowledge of nutrition and the environment can help determine healthy food choices
- discuss the kinds of factors that should be considered when making healthy food choices

Materials

Activity Sheet 11 for each student (See Blackline Masters section.)

Setting the Stage

Discuss briefly the questions on student page 47.

- **How can knowing about nutrition and the environment help you make healthy food choices?**

  Knowing what nutrients the body needs, where food comes from, and how packaging impacts the environment will lead to healthy food choices.

- **What kinds of factors should be considered when making healthy food choices?**

  Answers include number of servings, amount of added sugar and fat, information about nutrients, how the food is packaged, how the food production or packaging impacts the environment.

Focus

1. Have students brainstorm a list of food choices that are typically offered on campus. Encourage them to write down each food without stopping to evaluate its nutritional value. Once they have finished listing their options, they can focus on which combination of choices will be best. Remind students that they may discover more than one choice. They also can consider how foods go together and the importance of varying foods to choose a balanced meal. For example, brown rice may be a healthy choice for a side dish, but if you have chosen a tuna sandwich on whole-wheat bread for the main dish, it would be better to balance it with vegetables or fruit on the side. Explanations for students' choices can be recorded in the Notes section of the activity sheet.

2. Have students complete work on Activity Sheet 11.

It's a Wrap

In a class discussion, ask students what they have learned about making food choices on campus. Have them discuss how making healthy food choices means changing habits. What strategies can they use to make new habits stick?

Home

Follow-Up Invite several volunteers to discuss the packaging they found at home. What alternatives can they think of to reduce waste? How can packaging influence what they buy? When is a sack inside of a box inside of a wrapper necessary?

Assignment Home activity on student page 48.

Brainstorm a list of possible ways to reduce packaging waste at home. Evaluate which ideas will work and which will not. Give reasons for your ideas.

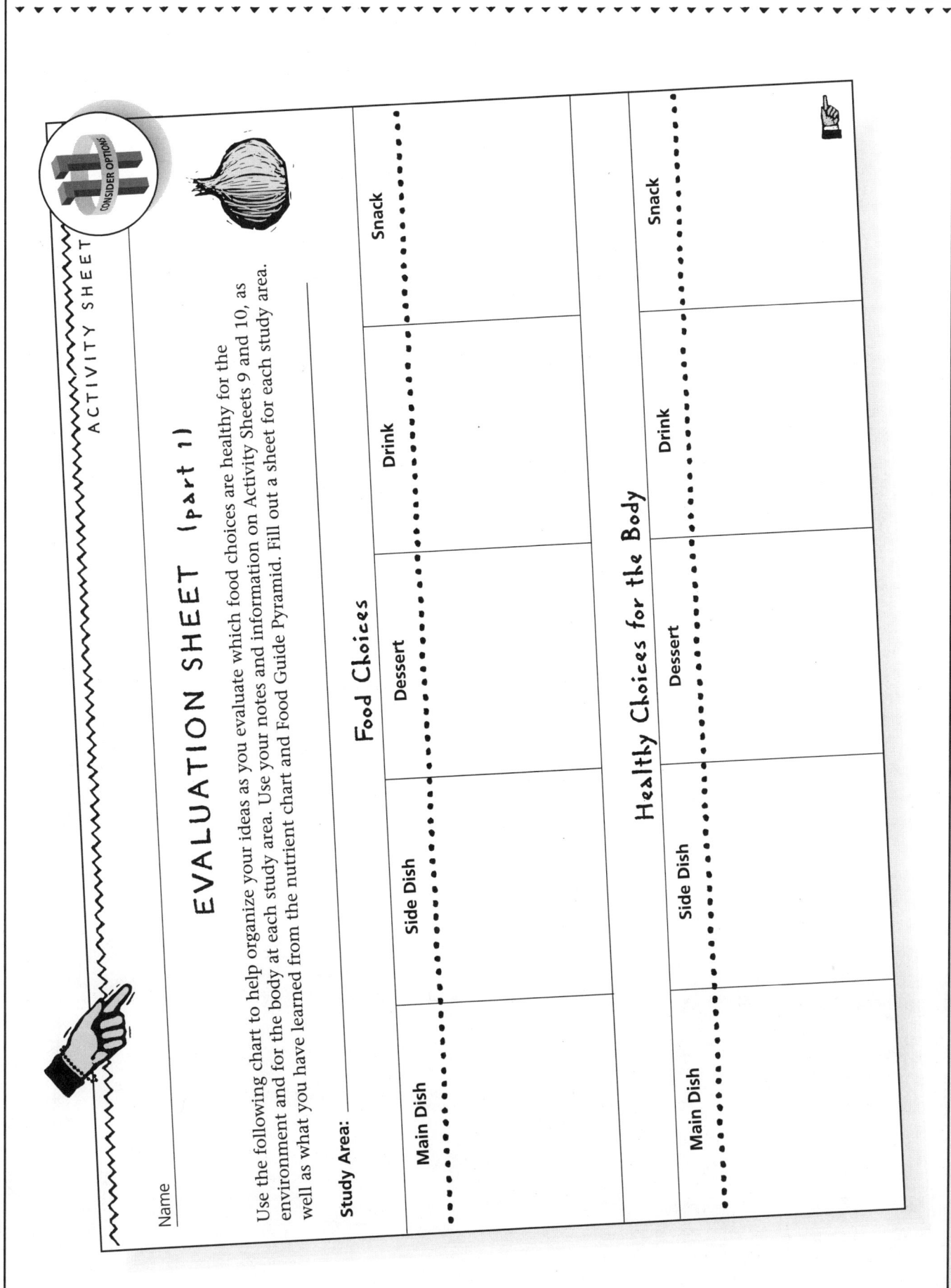

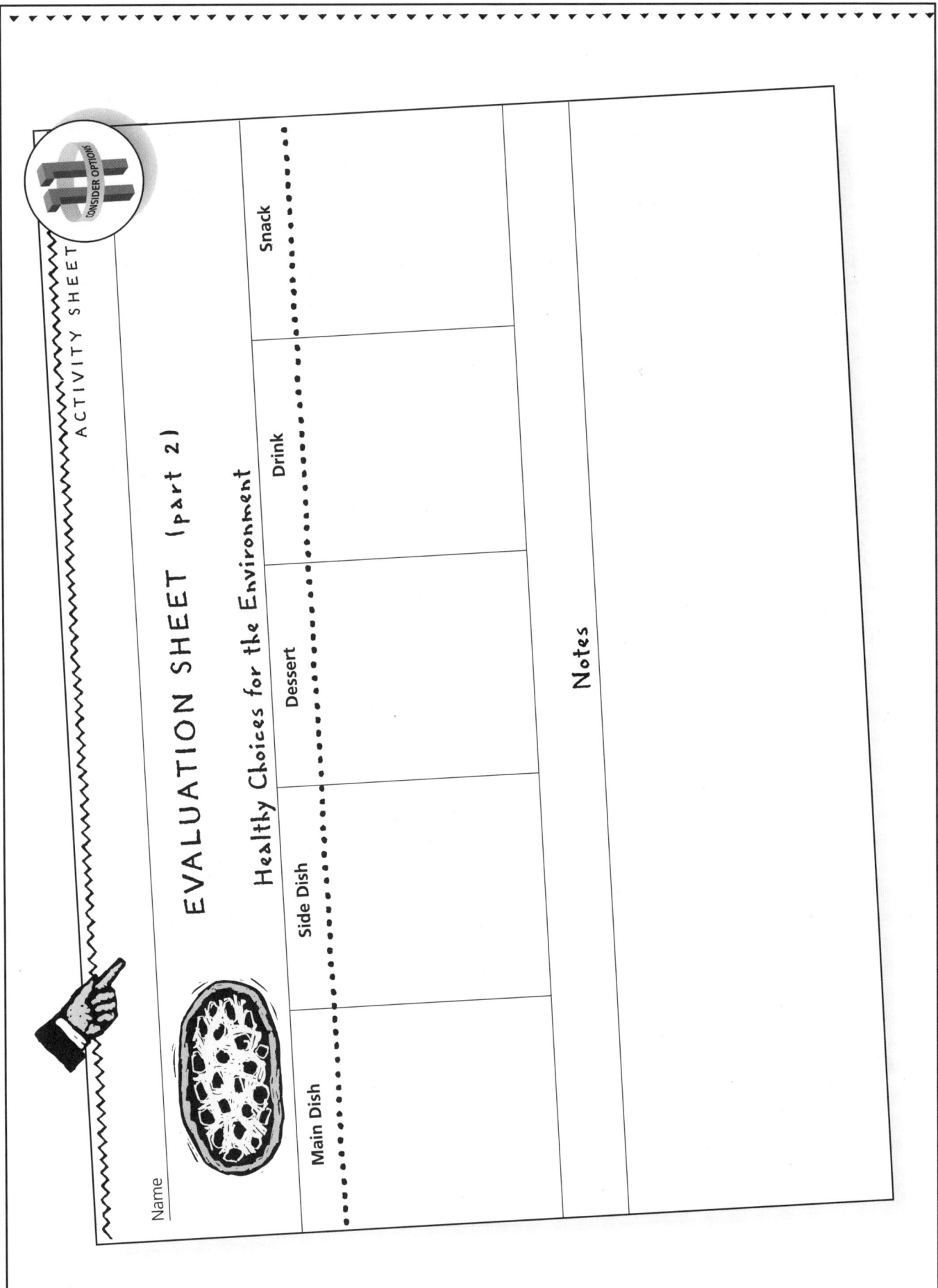

ACTIVITY SHEET

EVALUATION SHEET (part 2)

Healthy Choices for the Environment

Name

Main Dish	Side Dish	Dessert	Drink	Snack

Notes

72 Environmental ACTION Food Teacher Resource Guide

WEIGH THE COSTS AND BENEFITS

Students will evaluate healthy food choices by analyzing their costs and benefits.

Objectives

After completing this activity, students will be able to
- evaluate the costs and benefits of healthy food choices
- explain the importance of considering both long- and short-term benefits in recommending food choices

Prepare

Before students begin the activity, you may want to discuss the different kinds of costs and benefits they should consider. Help students understand that not all costs or benefits are monetary. What steps will have to be taken to get students to change their habits? How long will the process take? How many are likely to cooperate? How can students be reminded to keep health and the environment in mind as they make food choices?

Materials

Activity Sheet 12 for each student

Setting the Stage

Discuss briefly the questions on student page 50.

- **Can you measure or put a value on nonmonetary costs and benefits that affect human health or the environment? Explain your answer.**

  Answers will vary. Students should recognize that many of these costs are not easily measured or quantified. They should also recognize the importance of nonmonetary costs and how they impact food choices.

- **Why is it important to consider both long- and short-term benefits when recommending food choices?**

  Both the costs and benefits may vary over time. A new strategy may appear costly in the short term but may result in significant long-term savings. The opposite can also be true. It is important to assess costs and benefits accurately in order to identify and measure these effects.

Focus

1. Students can use the following questions to guide them as they evaluate the costs and benefits of the food choices they recommend.
- What are the monetary costs? Do healthy choices cost more than unhealthy choices?
- What are the nonmonetary costs? How much does having an unhealthy body cost you?
- What are the hidden costs, if any? Do any nonmonetary costs translate to hidden costs?
- What are the benefits to the environment, quality of life, health, and so on?

2. Have students complete the work on Activity Sheet 12.

It's a Wrap

Review students' findings on Activity Sheet 12.
What are the short- and long-term benefits of changing one's eating habits to make choices that are healthy for the body and for the environment?

Home

Follow-Up Invite students to share their findings about packaging. How does storage impact food choices?

Assignment Home activity on student page 51.

Visit a local grocery store or convenience store. How do prices of unhealthy snacks and healthy snacks compare? Does juice cost more or less than soda? Does an apple cost more or less than a bag of chips? Make a chart to show your cost comparisons.

ACTIVITY SHEET 12
CONSIDER OPTIONS

Name

ASSESSING COSTS AND BENEFITS

Use the following chart to evaluate each healthy food choice you made on Activity Sheet 11.

	Costs	Benefits
Healthy Food Choices for the Body	Monetary: Nonmonetary:	Monetary: Nonmonetary:
Healthy Choices for the Environment	Monetary: Nonmonetary:	Monetary: Nonmonetary:

Consider Options: Weigh the Costs and Benefits 75

CONSIDER FOOD CHOICES AND CHANGES

Students have learned about the environmental and health considerations that come into play when making food choices, and they have weighed costs and benefits of each choice. Now they are ready to take all of these things into consideration as they make personal food choices and recommend changes to implement at school.

Objectives

After completing this activity, student will be able to

- specify personal food choices
- recommend healthy food choices that can be offered at school

Materials

Activity Sheet 13 for each student

Setting the Stage

Discuss briefly the questions on student page 53.

- **What should you consider when you make food choices?**

  Answers include how healthy the food is, how its production impacts the environment, how it is packaged, where it fits in the Food Guide Pyramid, what nutrients it provides, how it fits in with a balanced diet.

- **What are some of the benefits of making healthy food choices?**

  Healthy food choices may be environmentally friendly, may make you feel more alert and energetic, may be important for long-range health and quality of life.

Focus

1. Remind students of all the factors that go into making a healthy food choice. Discuss healthy food choices students would like to see offered at school, either in the cafeteria or in the vending machines. Be sure students take all of the criteria into account as they make their recommendations.

2. Have students complete work on Activity Sheet 13.

It's a Wrap

Discuss students' work on Activity Sheet 13. What habits will students have to change in order to make healthy choices on a regular basis? What healthy food choices did students want to see served at school?

Home

Follow-Up Have students discuss their snack food survey. Were they surprised by how much snack foods can cost? What snacks were most cost-effective?

Assignment Home activity on student page 54.

 Conduct a family snack survey. Find out what each family member likes to nibble on between meals, during TV time, or at movies or sporting events. Use what you have learned to evaluate your family's food choices. What are the healthiest snacks they have chosen? What healthy choices can you suggest? Record your findings in your Journal.

ACTIVITY SHEET 13 CONSIDER OPTIONS

Name

CHANGING FOOD HABITS (part 1)

Use the chart below to outline how you will change your habits in the food choices you make, taking into account health, the environment, and the costs and benefits of each change. Include notes about changes you would like to see.

Food Choices	For Me	For the School
Main Dishes		
Side Dishes		

78 Environmental ACTION Food Teacher Resource Guide

ACTIVITY SHEET 17

Name

CHANGING FOOD HABITS (part 2)

Food Choices	For Me	For the School
Desserts		
Drinks		
Snacks		

Consider Options: Consider Food Choices and Changes 79

ACT LOCALLY

Students can use the following outreach activities to apply their learning, share information, and strengthen their ties to the community.

1. Write a "Wrapper Rap" that you can present to schoolmates at a pep rally or an assembly. In the lyrics, focus on making food choices that do not have excess packaging to litter the campus. For example:

   *An apple is a tasty treat—
   Its package goes on the compost heap!
   It has a core and it has a stem,
   And they're both wrapped up in a bright
      red skin!
   A plastic sack? You can't eat that!
      Wrapper rap!*

2. Design a logo to silkscreen on a canvas shopping bag that will remind shoppers to make food choices that are healthy for their bodies and for the environment. Sell the bags through your school parent-teacher group.

3. Plan a schoolwide Frozen Yogurt Social that will feature healthy dessert choices, such as frozen yogurt with a variety of fruit toppings, fat-free cookies, nonfat drinks.

4. Create a display for the school lobby or hallway, featuring a healthy food choice collage made from wrappers and food packages picked up around campus.

Take Action

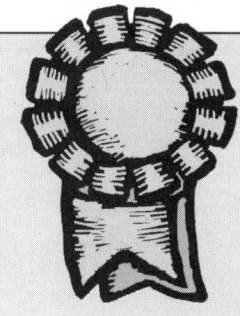

FOOD CHOICE RECOMMENDATIONS

Students have explored making healthy food choices, taking into account costs and benefits as well as environmental considerations. Have them work together in their Action Groups to recommend food choice changes they would like to see implemented on campus.

Objectives

At the end of this activity, students will be able to

- assess the feasibility of a recommended food change
- make recommendations based on a number of competing factors

Materials

Activity Sheet 14 for each student (See Blackline Masters section.)

Setting the Stage

Discuss briefly the questions on student page 59.

- **What do you need to consider in deciding what food choices you want to recommend?**

  Students should realize that cost and availability will be a major consideration; they should also think about how they will determine which item(s) to replace.

- **What criteria will you use to choose a recommendation?**

  Students will need to find ways to combine what they know about making choices that are healthy for their bodies and for the environment, as well as choices that will be cost-effective to serve at school, are not difficult to supply, and will be widely accepted.

Focus

1. Explain that now that students have evaluated their food choices, they can use what they have discovered to make a recommendation to the food service providers on campus. Once group members have decided on which food changes to recommend, discuss strategies for convincing their classmates.

2. Students will use Activity Sheet 14 to evaluate each Action Group's ideas.

It's a Wrap

Discuss some of the solutions that were given a low ranking. What factors compromised the effectiveness of the solution? How could the plans have been changed to be more successful over the short and long run?

Home

Follow-Up Discuss students' family snack surveys. What ideas do they have for encouraging family members to choose healthier snacks?

Assignment Home activity on student page 60.

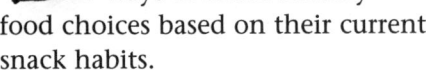 Write up a plan for recommending to family members (including yourself!) ways to make healthy food choices based on their current snack habits.

ACTIVITY SHEET

Name

RATING SHEET

Fill in the following rating sheet for each presentation.

Group

Plan

Costs

Expensive • • • Inexpensive

Health and Environmental Benefits

Low • • • High

Long-Term Effectiveness

Low • • • High

Difficulty of Implementing

Low • • • High

Cooperation Incentives

Low • • • High

Effectiveness of Presentation

Low • • • High

Additional Factors to Consider

_____

_____

_____

Priority

Low • • • High

Take Action: Food Choice Recommendations

PREPARE AND PRESENT PROPOSAL

Students will write a proposal for recommending healthy food choices at school. They will outline costs, benefits, and describe the ways to implement their recommendations. Then they will present the proposal to the school committee.

Objectives

After completing this activity, students will be able to
- assign tasks to complete a project
- use an outline to prepare a proposal

Prepare

Discuss the school committee for whom students will be preparing the proposal. Tell them who the members are and describe what you know about the process they will use to evaluate the proposal. You may want to set a date for meeting with the school committee that will be receiving the proposal package.

Materials

- Activity Sheet 15
- art materials

Setting the Stage

Discuss briefly the questions on student page 62.

- **What important problems were discovered during your food choice audit?**

  Responses include specific instances of excess packaging, wasted food, unhealthy choices, limited choices.

- **How will the healthy food choices you are proposing provide both short- and long-term benefits?**

  Students should suggest ways to cut down on litter, cut down on waste, increase nutritional options, change personal habits, improve overall health, conserve natural resources.

- **What were the most important reasons for choosing these recommendations?**

  Possible answers include the nutritional value of the recommended food choice, packaging considerations, availability, cost, popularity with students.

Focus

Lead students in a brainstorming session to explore ways of organizing and presenting their proposal.

- **What will be the most effective plan for organizing the presentation? Should you begin with the criticism, provide the recommendation, and then outline the benefits? Would another approach be more persuasive?**

  Students may debate different organizational plans, all of which may be reasonable. Students should consider their audience (the committee) and decide how they can best capture its attention and gain its approval.

- **What is the most important idea you want to emphasize? Nutrition? Packaging? Benefits?**

  Students will realize that there are many beneficial ideas included in their proposal, but guide them to understand that a persuasive proposal will be more effective if it is well researched, documented, and presented.

86   Environmental ACTION   Food   Teacher Resource Guide

- **How can you use charts, graphs, tables, and diagrams to illustrate and promote your ideas?**

  Students should suggest ways of displaying information using graphic organizers. They might show how all of the foods offered in the vending machine fit into the Food Guide Pyramid and highlight how their food choice will provide balance and important nutrients, how their recommendation will cut down on litter and waste, how their recommendation is likely to be received by the study body.

- **What tone will be the most persuasive?**

  Students should consider what approach will be both diplomatic and credible to the committee members. For example, write the following two statements on the board and guide students in examining which is the most effective and why.

  Mr. Fritter Apple Dumplings taste revolting, which is why they rot in the machines or get thrown on the ground along with their plastic wrappers.

  Mr. Fritter Apple Dumplings can be replaced by fresh apples from Granny Smith farms at half the cost and without added sugar or fat.

  Invite students to suggest additions or revisions to the outline on the student page. Then have students divide up the tasks and responsibilities and proceed with preparing their proposal.

It's a Wrap

When students have completed their proposal, allow time for them to reflect on their work and to revise parts of it as necessary before delivering it or presenting it to the committee for consideration.

Reminder At this time you may wish to administer the Content Quiz and Student Survey. Your students may already have taken these as pre-tests. They may now be given as post-tests. In addition, the Student Self-Evaluation Form can now be used to help students assess their own progress. These forms are all included in the Blackline Masters/Assessment Tools section of your Resource Guide. Answers to the Content Quiz are on page 16.

Home

Follow-Up Invite students to tell how their families reacted to the snack suggestions.

Assignment Home activity on student page 63.

Make a small poster to hang on your refrigerator at home, reminding family members to make healthy food choices as they reach for a bite to eat.

ACTIVITY SHEET 15 TAKE ACTION

Name

 **PROPOSAL CHECKLIST (part 1)**

Use this checklist to plan and monitor tasks that may need to be done in order to complete your proposal. Make a note of who is responsible for completing each task, when each task should be completed, materials needed, and so on. Add to the list as needed.

TASKS	NOTES
1. TITLE ☐ Cover illustration ☐ Proposal statement	
2. WRITE THE INTRODUCTORY PARAGRAPH. ☐ Explain the project. ☐ Briefly describe audit results.	
3. WRITE YOUR RECOMMENDATIONS. ☐ Describe your plan. ☐ Highlight the benefits. ☐ Specify the costs. ☐ Suggest a step-by-step implementation schedule. ☐ Include ideas for motivating student body, increasing awareness, and encouraging participation (if applicable).	

Continue your recommendations on next page.

88   Environmental ACTION   Food   Teacher Resource Guide

ACTIVITY SHEET

Name

PROPOSAL CHECKLIST (part 2)

TASKS	NOTES
(CONTINUED)	
4. PRESENT YOUR RESEARCH FINDINGS. ☐ Prepare graphs. ☐ Design tables or charts. ☐ Prepare illustrations, photographs, or other art works.	
5. WRITE YOUR CLOSING STATEMENT. ☐ Outline aspects of the proposal that are already underway and explain where you go from here.	

Take Action: Prepare and Present Proposal 89

TRACK RESPONSES TO RECOMMENDATIONS

Students will follow up on their healthy food choice proposal as it is implemented on campus. They will work to increase awareness of nutrition and environmental considerations in order to begin changing the habits of the student body and staff.

Objectives

After completing this activity, students will be able to

- summarize food choice recommendations approved by the school committee and track their implementation
- survey and assess awareness of nutrition and how healthy food choices relate to the environment

Prepare

Review the school committee's response to the food choice recommendations students proposed and monitor measures taken. Establish a way to track success and to continue advocacy of healthy food choices. Activity Sheet 16 can be used as a guide.

Materials

Activity Sheet 16 for each student

Setting the Stage

Discuss briefly the questions on student page 65.

- **How can you find out what effect your food choice recommendations are having?**

  Responses may include monitoring the vending machines and cafeteria lines, interviewing food service and maintenance providers about food and packaging waste and disposal.

- **How can you assess the level of nutrition and environmental awareness and the amount of participation?**

  Responses may include making observations about changes in personal eating habits, interviewing schoolmates, interviewing food service providers.

Focus

Discuss the effects students observe as they see their food choice recommendations implemented. Encourage them to evaluate the impact their work is having on changing people's eating habits.

- **How can other students and staff in your school be motivated to make healthy food choices?**

  Encourage students to brainstorm methods to keep nutrition and related issues before the student body. Examples might include updates in the student newspaper or a student survey.

- **How can student participation in making healthy food choices be increased?**

  Challenge students to think of ways to continue promoting the importance of making healthy food choices. Ideas might include organizing a committee to produce regular nutrition posters, declaring a quarterly "You Are What You Eat" day at school, creating a forum in the school newspaper where all students can contribute ideas or recipes that incorporate healthy food choices, staging on-going health awareness activities.

It's a Wrap

Discuss responses to It's a Wrap questions and the ongoing success of students' healthy food choices plan.

- **What are the most surprising benefits of your recommendations?**

    Possible responses include the amount of savings, the degree of support shown by students and faculty, the enthusiasm of the school committee.

- **What would make the recommendations more effective?**

    Now that students are seeing the effects of their plan, they should have additional ideas to improve or expand it.

    Challenge students to list more ideas for increasing student awareness of making healthy food choices.

Home

Follow-Up Encourage volunteers to describe or share the poster they made for their families.

Assignment Home activity on the student page 66.

Write a progress report in your Journal. Think about how your own eating habits have changed as a result of learning more about nutrition. What is the hardest thing about changing unhealthy eating habits? What is the most rewarding thing about changing unhealthy eating habits?

ACTIVITY SHEET 16 TAKE ACTION

Name

TRACKING SHEET (part 1)

Use this tracking sheet to summarize and monitor the results of your healthy food choice recommendations.

Recommendation

Implementation Report

Month 1

Month 2

ACTIVITY SHEET 16 TAKE ACTION

Name _____

TRACKING SHEET (part 2)

Month 3

Participation Rating

Low • — • — • High

Impact on Personal Food Choices

Low • — • — • High

Recommended Changes or Modifications

Take Action: Track Responses to Recommendations 93

Appendices

Section A
FOOD PRODUCTION PRACTICES AND THE ENVIRONMENT

"Nothing links us more powerfully to the earth—to its rivers and soils and its seasons of plenty—than food. It is a daily reminder of our connection to the miracle of life. Little wonder, then, that most of the world's religions require consecration of food before it is transformed into the stuff of our lives."

Albert Gore, *Earth in the Balance*,
Houghton Mifflin, 1992, p. 126

Most of us sit down to a meal without thinking much about how we may be impacting the environment, but ecological issues touch our lives perhaps most directly in our daily food choices. The nutrition that sustains us comes from the environment—from the sun and the earth's water and soil. It reaches us through the foods we eat, which come from plants or animals raised on farms and ranches.

In the last 50 years, many effective techniques for raising foods have been developed. Food production has been increased in order to meet the demands of a growing population and increased demand in western and industrialized countries for more foods from animals (meats, eggs, and dairy products).

As with any business trying new techniques, some of these farm production practices have not been perfect. Farmers are the first to understand the importance of protecting the earth's land and water, but some of the farming practices that have dramatically increased food production are now being seen to have harmful effects on the environment. Outlined below are some of the environmental problems related to food production practices. Methods farmers are now using to correct these harmful effects will be discussed later.

Soil Erosion The top layer of soil, called topsoil, contains precious microorganisms and nutrients that make the soil fertile for growing crops. When steep slopes are cultivated, when plant cover is removed by animals' overgrazing or by cultivation, or when land is improperly irrigated, topsoil can be carried away by wind or washed away by water. The worldwide loss of topsoil from erosion from cropland may be as high as 25 billion tons each year. Topsoil is also depleted of its nutrients when large amounts of the same crop are grown year after year in the same field. Nature cannot replace topsoil at anywhere near the rate at which it is being lost—scientists estimate that it takes something like 5000 years for the earth to produce five inches of topsoil.

Desertification Desertification is the creation of desert-like land, unsuitable for farming, from previously fertile land. Continual erosion causes desertification, generally by human misuse or overuse of land mainly through overgrazing by livestock and deforestation for fuelwood. Growing techniques that force heavy crop growth (overcultivation) on land that is not particularly fertile and improper irrigation are also causes of desertification. Possibly as much as 20 percent of the land in the U.S. has undergone or is threatened by desertification. Research in the late 1980s showed that worldwide an area of cropland the size of the state of Kansas is lost to desertification each year.

Loss of Habitat and Loss of Biodiversity More and more land has been cleared of natural plant and animal ecosystems to create cropland and grazing land. In some places, this is a major cause of loss of forests (deforestation). One estimate suggests that about seven times more acreage of forest in the U.S. is cleared for grazing livestock and growing feed for livestock than is cleared for development. Development, of course, creates the need for new lands to be cleared for farms as cities, industries, and highways take over some of the best agricultural land. When land is cleared of trees or other natural vegetation, the entire habitat and all the wildlife of that ecosystem—its biodiversity—are lost.

Water Use and Water Pollution Water is a precious and limited resource. Irrigation of cropland and raising livestock are the major uses of water in the U.S. and worldwide. About 80 percent of U.S. water use is for agriculture (over 90 percent is used for irrigation in some dry states). Almost half of the water is used to raise livestock, including growing the grains and beans to feed the animals. The major cause of water pollution in the U.S. is from polluted water running off farmland. This water carries chemical fertilizers, pesticides, topsoil, animal waste, and salts from soil and irrigation water.

Energy Use Technological advances have allowed us to grow foods in great quantity in the regions where they grow best, store them for longer periods of time, and transport them long distances to the consumer. Many of these techniques require high uses of energy for chemicals, farm machinery, food processing, storage, packaging, and transportation. Fertilizers and pesticides used to grown abundant crops are made using petroleum. Since the mid-40s, the amount of energy used for each acre of farmland in the U.S. has increased fourfold. Some studies show that in the U.S., energy equaling about 150 gallons of oil is used for each acre of crops produced and that food processing and packaging consume about six percent of all energy used.

Pesticide Use The use of pesticides in agriculture has increased greatly since 1950 and has helped to increase food production. However, many serious problems are associated with the use of pesticides. Pesticides are poisons, and they kill not only the insect or plant they were intended to kill but harmless plants and animals as well. Many pesticides have been linked to various human diseases. For this reason, the government regulates the use of pesticides in the U.S. Pesticides have also caused serious problems in polluting water, soil, and air. In addition, pesticide use has too often back-fired—insects adapt and become resistant to a pesticide used to kill them or resistant insects that were not previously on a crop move in and become major pests. Pesticides that have been banned in the U.S. are still used in other countries and reach the U.S. in imported produce and other foods and in air and water pollution. Some people choose to avoid foods grown with pesticides by purchasing organic or pesticide-free foods.

Packaging Waste The amount of packaging used for foods has increased as more processed or prepared foods are produced, as food producers rely on packages to attract consumers, and as foods are stored and transported long distances. Some food packaging can be recycled, but much of it winds up in landfills, contributing greatly to the worldwide problem of waste disposal. In addition, production of packaging uses a lot of resources such as energy, water, trees, and fossil fuels.

Genetic Engineering Scientists are using genetic engineering to develop new food crops. This process is the altering of the genes of a living organism to change its characteristics. For example, a new tomato has been engineered that will stay fresh longer. This practice is still relatively new and, while it promises some better products, many people feel concern about the unknown long-term effects on humans or other animals and plants in the earth's ecosystems.

Livestock Although there is much debate on this topic, many environmentalists and researchers suggest that eating less meat is one of the main actions we can take to help the environment. The reason they make this suggestion is because raising animals for food consumes large amounts of land, water, energy, and grain. Range-fed livestock can cause environmental problems when they are allowed to overgraze land; grain-fed livestock consume large resources of grain and soybeans. In addition, many people feel concern about inhumane treatment of animals raised for food and about possible human health hazards of hormones and medicines given to animals. Here are some of the points made about resource use, the environment, and livestock:

- More than two-thirds of land used for agriculture in the U.S. is used to raise livestock or for growing livestock feed.
- More than half the water used in the U.S. goes to raising livestock or their feed; producing a pound of meat consumes 100 times more water than growing a pound of wheat.
- Producing a pound of grain-fed beef requires over 20 times the energy (including the energy used to grow their feed) required to grow a nutritionally equal amount of grain or beans.
- U.S. livestock consume enough grain and soybeans to support more than five times the nation's human population.
- Livestock waste accounts for twice as much water pollution as industry.
- Clearing land for raising livestock and overgrazing by livestock are important causes of deforestation, soil erosion, and desertification.

Eating fewer animal products may help the environment and, as described in later Information and Issues sections, promotes good health as well. Recognizing this fact, Americans as a nation have in fact reduced their intake of meats, especially red meats, in recent years.

Sustainable Agriculture

Farmers in the U.S. and in many other countries are beginning to use methods of food production that minimize harm to the environment. These methods are called "sustainable" because they sustain the environment for future generations. The principles of sustainable agriculture include

- using minimum amounts of water and energy
- eliminating or minimizing use of chemical fertilizers
- eliminating or minimizing use of chemical pesticides
- growing plants appropriate to the region (considering soil type and climate)
- using seeds that promote genetic diversity (nonhybrids and multiple varieties)
- protecting topsoil by using appropriate drainage and watering systems

Section B
THE FOOD GUIDE PYRAMID

The Food Guide Pyramid was developed by the U.S. Department of Agriculture (USDA) in 1992 to illustrate the guidelines for a healthy diet for Americans. The pyramid shows how much to eat each day from each of five basic food groups to get the nutrients we need. Because the typical American diet contains too much fat and sugar, the pyramid also focuses attention on the importance of keeping intake of fats and sugars low.

Why a Pyramid?

The pyramid shape was chosen because it is the best to convey three basic principles of a healthy diet:

- Proportion—Foods from different groups are needed in different proportions. The foundation of a healthy diet is a large amount of grains (bread, cereal, etc.) and relatively large amounts of fruits and vegetables. Smaller amounts of foods are needed from the meat and dairy food groups.
- Moderation—Fats, oils, and sweets are to be used only in moderation.
- Variety—Because different foods provide different nutrients, no one food group is more important than another. As the pyramid shows, we need a variety of foods from the five major food groups each day.

Different Needs for Different People

The Food Guide Pyramid presents ranges of recommended numbers of servings for each food group. Teenagers and active adults generally need more nutrients, and thus greater numbers of servings, than do older or more inactive people. Men generally need more than women. Very active people, such as athletes or laborers, need more servings, as do women who are pregnant. A chart of the number of servings recommended for people of different ages and activity levels is presented in the Explore 2 activity.

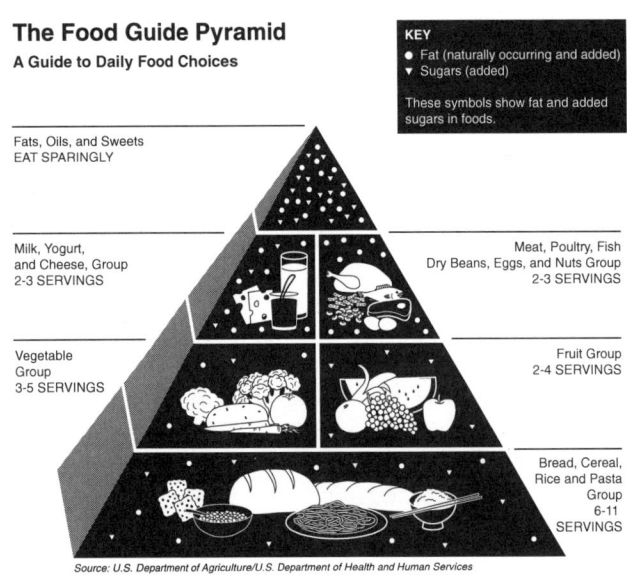

What Is a Serving?

A "serving" on the Food Guide Pyramid is not the same as a "helping" of food at home, at school, or in a restaurant. In general, a serving is smaller than a typical helping or portion. Many foods provide a combination of servings from several different groups. For example, a generous serving of cheese pizza might count as 1 bread group serving (crust), 1 milk group serving (cheese), and about $\frac{1}{2}$ vegetable group serving (tomato sauce).

Below are listed some common foods and what counts as one serving. Use this list as a guide to help you estimate the number of servings in different meals.

Bread Group

(Eat 6–11 servings daily.)
- 1 slice of bread—white, whole-wheat, French, raisin, etc. (equals 1 oz)
- $\frac{1}{2}$ English muffin, bagel, or hamburger bun
- 1 pancake
- 1 6-inch tortilla
- 2 breadsticks
- 3–4 small crackers (rye crisps, saltines)
- $\frac{1}{2}$ cup cooked rice or pasta
- $\frac{1}{2}$ cup cooked grains (bulgur, millet, quinoa, barley)
- 1 oz ready-to-eat breakfast cereal
- 1 medium muffin*
- 1 oz pound cake*
- $\frac{1}{2}$ medium doughnut or croissant*
- $\frac{1}{6}$ piece of 8-inch, two-crust pie*

Vegetable Group

(Eat 3–5 servings daily.)
- 1 cup raw, leafy vegetables (lettuce, spinach, kale, beet greens)
- $\frac{1}{2}$ cup nonleafy, chopped vegetables (raw or cooked)
- $\frac{1}{2}$ cup canned or frozen vegetables
- 1 small baked potato (3 oz)
- 1 of corn on the cob (6 inches long)
- 1 tomato
- 3–5 broccoli spears
- 7–8 baby carrots or carrot sticks
- $\frac{1}{4}$ avocado*
- $\frac{3}{4}$ cup vegetable juice
- $\frac{1}{2}$ cup potato salad or scalloped potatoes*
- 10 French fries*

Fruit Group

(Eat 2–4 servings daily.)
- 1 medium whole fruit (apple, orange, banana, peach)
- 2 plums
- 3 apricots
- 12 cherries
- 15 grapes
- $\frac{1}{2}$ grapefruit
- $\frac{1}{2}$ cup chopped fruit
- $\frac{1}{2}$ cup raspberries, blackberries, strawberries
- $\frac{1}{4}$ cup dried fruit
- $\frac{3}{4}$ cup fruit juice

Milk Group

(Eat 2–3 servings daily.)
- 1 cup milk (skim, low-fat, whole*, chocolate*, buttermilk*)
- 1 cup yogurt (nonfat, low-fat, plain, flavored*, or frozen*)
- $\frac{1}{2}$ cup ricotta cheese*
- 2 cups cottage cheese*
- $1\frac{1}{2}$ cups ice cream* or ice milk*
- 10 oz milk shake*
- 2 oz process cheese*
- $1\frac{1}{2}$ oz natural cheese* (cheddar, mozzarella, etc.)

Meat Group

(Eat 2–3 servings daily for a total of 5–7 ounces.)
- 3 oz cooked poultry, ham, beef*
- 3 oz fish or shellfish (15 medium shrimp, 6 scallops or clams)*
- 4–6 slices bologna*
- 1 to $1\frac{1}{2}$ cups dry beans and peas, cooked

2–3 eggs*
4–6 Tbs peanut butter*
$\frac{2}{3}$ to 1 cup nuts*

Note: $\frac{1}{2}$ cup of cooked dry beans, 1 egg, or 2 tablespoons of peanut butter count as 1 ounce of lean meat

*Depending on the specific product, these foods may be very high in fat, sugar, and/or cholesterol and should be eaten in moderation and balanced in the overall diet with low-fat, low-sugar, and low-cholesterol items. See sections C and E for more information.

Fats, Oils, and Sweets

(Eat sparingly.)
    Butter, margarine (1 teaspoon or 1 pat = 5 grams of fat)
    Mayonnaise
    Salad dressing
    Cream cheese, sour cream, whipped cream
    Syrup, honey, sugar
    Jams, jellies
    Cola and other sweetened soft drinks
    Fruit drinks, lemonade, and so on
    Candy, chocolate
    Sherbet, sorbet, gelatin dessert

What the Pyramid Doesn't Tell Us

The Food Pyramid is a very useful guide for healthy meal planning, but nutritionists and the USDA point out that other factors need to be emphasized as well. Other important guidelines include the following:

- In bread group choices, select whole-grain breads and cereals.
- In milk group choices, select low-fat or nonfat dairy products.
- In meat group choices, select lean meats. Eat dry beans, peas, and lentils often—they provide the protein of the meat group and are low in fat and high in fiber.
- In vegetable and fruit group choices, regularly select dark green leafy vegetables, vegetables from the cabbage family (turnips, broccoli, cabbage, cauliflower), deep-yellow vegetables, and Vitamin C-rich fruits and vegetables.
- Use all fats and sweets sparingly, but particularly limit saturated fats. (They are found in meat and dairy products and some vegetable oils such as coconut and palm oil.)
- Drink 6 to 10 glasses of water each day.

Section C provides further information on these and other nutritional guidelines.

The 5-A-Day Campaign

The Food Guide Pyramid recommends eating 5–9 servings of fruits and vegetables each day. A 1991 government study found that Americans on average eat only 2–3 servings a day. Because many research studies have pointed to fruits and vegetables (including dried beans and peas) as important in reducing the risk of heart disease, birth defects, and cancer, the government has launched a 5-A-Day Campaign to educate the public and encourage increased intake of these foods. The campaign is also providing helpful ideas about ways to include more fruits and vegetables in the diet. Watch for the 5-A-Day message in grocery stores, on television, in churches and community centers, on food labels, and elsewhere.

Section C
NUTRITION BASICS

What people choose to eat depends on a great many factors—family traditions, health concerns, environmental concerns, economic concerns, and taste preferences. In most western, industrialized countries today, people have an incredible variety of foods from which to choose. As a trend, however, over the last hundred years people in these societies have developed dietary habits that have not promoted good health.

Researchers have found the typical western diet to be linked with an increase in certain diseases, particularly some heart diseases, some cancers, obesity, and diabetes. This diet is

- high in meats and fat (especially saturated fat), cholesterol, and salt
- higher in calories than the body needs
- low in grains, vegetables, fruit, and fiber

It has included fewer natural, unrefined foods and many more processed foods that tend to be high in fat, sugar, salt, and preservatives.

The good news is that in recent years more and more people in Western societies are becoming informed about health and nutrition and are combining healthier diets with proper exercise to maintain health and fitness. They are learning that a healthy diet not only reduces the risk of diseases but also helps them to work productively and feel good. It helps children to grow and do well in school. Moreover, they are discovering that there are many inviting and delicious ways to combine foods to make a healthy diet.

To help people know what to eat to stay healthy, the USDA suggests these guidelines for Americans two years of age and older:

Dietary Guidelines for Americans

1. Eat a variety of foods.
2. Maintain a healthy weight.
3. Choose a diet low in fat, saturated fat, and cholesterol.
4. Choose a diet with plenty of vegetables, fruits, and grain products.
5. Use sugars only in moderation.
6. Use salt and sodium only in moderation.
7. Children and adolescents should not drink alcoholic beverages.

These are the guidelines illustrated by the Food Guide Pyramid. They help us get the necessary nutrients for good health.

What Are Nutrients?

Nutrients are the chemical substances that foods provide. They give the body the energy it needs, the materials for body building or repair, and the ability to maintain a healthy metabolism. Nutrients are generally classified into six groups: water, carbohydrates, proteins, fats, minerals, and vitamins. Minerals and vitamins are needed in small amounts but are essential to good health. Carbohydrates, fats, and proteins provide energy and are needed in larger amounts.

The Essential Nutrients

Water Water is probably the most important nutrient. A person can live without other nutrients for several weeks or even months but cannot live without water for longer than about a week. All body functions require water. It is also the nutrient we need in the greatest quantity. Adults need about $2\frac{1}{2}$ quarts of water each day in the form of water in foods and beverages (about $\frac{1}{3}$ of the water we need comes from the water in foods). Beverages such as juice, soft drinks, coffee, and tea actually take water from the body rather than supplying it. That's why you may still feel thirsty after drinking them. It is recommended that a person drink six to ten glasses of plain water each day.

Carbohydrates Carbohydrates are the body's main source of energy. They come from plant foods and include all sugars and starches:

- Sugars (or "simple carbohydrates") are digested quickly and supply short bursts of energy. Sugars are found in many foods, especially fruits, honey, syrups, white or brown sugar, and molasses. (See section E for more information about sugars.)
- Starches (or "complex carbohydrates") take longer to digest than sugars and thus supply energy for a longer period of time. The main sources of starches are foods such as grains, breads, cereals, pastas, potatoes, and beans. Different starches have long been the basis of diets around the world—rice in Asia, wheat in the Middle East, corn and potatoes in the Americas. A common mistake people make is thinking that starches are fattening. Starches in fact are not fattening at all. It is what is put on them—additions such as butter, sour cream, cheese, oil, and cream—that can be fattening. As the Food Guide Pyramid recommends, a healthy diet includes more starches than any other foods.

Fiber Fiber is plant material made of complex carbohydrates that cannot be digested. Because it is not absorbed by the body, it moves food through the stomach and intestines. It is essential in our diets for this purpose. Research indicates that eating enough fiber reduces the risk of certain cancers and intestinal problems. Many Americans' diets contain too little fiber. Good sources of fiber are whole-grain breads and cereals, cooked dried beans and peas (such as lentils, pintos, chick peas, kidney beans, split peas), vegetables, and fruits.

Proteins Proteins are the primary source of building materials for the body. Muscle, skin, hair, and cartilage, for example, are made of proteins. In addition, like carbohydrates and fats, proteins provide energy for the body. Meat, cheese, eggs, fish, and milk are animal sources of protein. Beans, peas, and nuts are the richest plant sources of protein. Grains are also an important source of proteins.

Proteins are made of smaller components called amino acids. Animal foods provide what are called complete proteins that contain all the amino acids essential to human health. Plant foods provide incomplete proteins because they lack certain amino acids, but eaten in combination they provide complete proteins. For example, grains with beans provide complete proteins, as do beans with nuts and seeds or grains and leafy vegetables with nuts and seeds. These foods do not have to be eaten together in the same meal in order to provide complete protein. Although many people feel concern that a vegetarian diet does not provide enough protein, it is easy to get enough protein without animal products in a healthy diet that includes a variety of foods. Vegetarians need to be careful, however, to get enough of the essential vitamins and minerals.

The amount of protein needed daily is estimated to be between 45 and 65 grams, with children needing more than adults. Most Americans eat at least twice this much. Although some reports have suggested that eating too much protein may contribute to kidney damage, bone problems, or other diseases, this is not certain. Studies do indicate, however, that a diet high in protein from animal sources can lead to heart disease because of the high amounts of fat and cholesterol (a fat-like substance) in animal products.

For most Americans, there are two challenges in regard to protein in the diet. The first challenge is to limit daily intake of meats and poultry to the recommended two or three three-ounce servings (see section B, Food Guide Pyramid). A rule of thumb to remember is that a three-ounce serving of meat is about the size of a deck of cards. The second challenge is to limit intake of protein from sources that are high-fat and high-cholesterol (whole milk, cheese, eggs, beef, pork, lamb, nuts, and seeds).

The chart below, based on the Food Guide Pyramid, gives you an idea of how much protein you get from different food groups.

Fats Fats include liquid oils and solid fats. They are a highly concentrated source of energy, and they enable the body to use certain essential vitamins. Fats that are not used to provide energy are stored in the body's fat cells.

There are three types of fats: saturated, monounsaturated, and polyunsaturated. Our bodies can make the saturated and monounsaturated fats that we need, but we need to eat some polyunsaturated fats. Polyunsaturated fats are easy to obtain from vegetable oils (safflower, sunflower, corn, sesame, soybean, and cottonseed) and from cold-water fish such as salmon, mackerel, or tuna. Monounsaturated fats are found in olive, peanut, and canola oils and in poultry, almonds, and some fish such as haddock. Saturated fats are found in largest amounts in fats from meat and dairy products. They are also found in chocolate and some vegetable oils such as coconut, palm, and palm kernel.

Reducing fat in the American diet is a much-publicized idea today. The main reason is that eating too much fat, particularly saturated fat, increases the risk of heart disease (the number one killer of Americans over 40). It also increases the risk of difficulties with weight control, symptoms of diseases such as multiple sclerosis, and some cancers.

The Dietary Guidelines recommend that we get no more than 30 percent of our daily calories from fat, and no more than 10 percent from saturated fat. On average, Americans obtain about 37 percent of their calories from fat. (See page 107 for information about calorie intake and section E for more information on reducing fat in the diet.)

Fats and oils add to the enjoyment of foods—studies show that people almost always choose foods with the most fat as the best tasting. Fats also satisfy hunger because they slow down the rate of digestion. A built-in preference for fat ensures that we get enough energy-providing

Food and Protein

Food Group	Serving Size	Grams of Protein	Number of Servings Per Day	Total Protein
Fruits & Vegetables	½ cup	0–2	5–9	0–18 grams
Grains & Cereals	½ cup	2	6–11	12–22 grams
Meat, eggs, beans	3 ounces	21	2–3	42–63 grams
Milk	8 ounces	8	2–3	16–24 grams
Daily Total				70–127 grams

Source: Nancy Anne DuPuy and Virginia Lee Mermel, *Focus on Nutrition*, Mosby-Year Book, Inc., 1995

foods, but we use much less energy in our lifestyles today and have much more food available than our ancestors did. Nutritionists point out that it is not necessary or even wise to give up all fats, but they should be eaten sparingly and balanced with greater amounts of low-fat foods.

Minerals Minerals are chemical elements that plants absorb from the soil and water. Animals obtain minerals by eating plants (and other plant-eating animals). They are essential in small amounts for the structure, growth, and functioning of the human body. The minerals that are required in greatest quantity in people's diets, called the major minerals, include calcium, phosphorus, magnesium, chloride, potassium, sodium, and sulfur. Calcium is well-known for its essential role in forming bones and teeth. It is also important for blood clotting. Other minerals, called trace minerals, are needed in very small quantities. Trace minerals include iron, fluoride, zinc, copper, and selenium. These minerals are as essential as the major minerals. Iron, for example, is an important part of blood. Manganese and zinc are needed for the healthy functioning of various chemical reactions in the body.

Eating a diet that contains a variety of unrefined foods is the best way to get an adequate amount of the needed minerals. In particular, we need plenty of whole foods, especially grains, fruits, and vegetables, along with small amounts of food from the milk and meat groups. Sodium (salt) is a mineral that most Americans eat in too great a quantity. A chart of the essential minerals, the foods that supply them, and their uses in the human body is presented in the Explore 4 activity.

Vitamins Vitamins are substances found in plant and animal foods that are essential in minute amounts to regulate the chemical reactions in the human body. Thirteen vitamins are currently known to be necessary for growth and health: Vitamin A, the B-complex vitamins (there are eight of these), and Vitamins C, D, E, and K. In order to use Vitamins A, D, E, and K, some fat must be included in the diet.

Vitamins are obtained by eating a diet that includes a variety of foods from each of the food groups. Whole, unprocessed foods contain the most vitamins, especially vegetables, fruits, and whole grain products. To get the essential vitamins, nutritionists advise us to eat the following:

- five servings of fruits and vegetables each day
- at least one Vitamin A-rich food each day
- at least one Vitamin C-rich food each day
- at least one serving of cabbage-family vegetables every other day

Vitamins are extremely important for human health. Some are associated with prevention of disease: for example, eating fruits and vegetables high in Vitamin C has been associated with a reduction in the occurrence of certain cancers and heart disease. Not getting enough of some vitamins is also associated with disease: a lack of Vitamin A can cause blindness, lack of Vitamin D can cause a skeletal disease called rickets, lack of Vitamin C can result in a disease called scurvy. Too much of some vitamins can cause disease, as well. A healthy diet will never result in too much of any vitamins, but taking large doses of vitamin supplements or eating too many vitamin-fortified foods can cause a harmful vitamin excess. A chart of the essential vitamins, the foods that supply them, and how they are used in the body is presented in the Explore 4 activity.

How Processing and Preparation Affect Nutrients

Refining and processing foods tends to decrease their valuable nutrient content. For example, whole grains are refined to make white flour. This process removes the parts of the grain that provide the most fiber, vitamins, and minerals. Because of this loss in nutrients, the government requires refined flours to have some of the vitamins and minerals added back. Products with vitamins or minerals added are said to be enriched or fortified. Generally enriching or fortifying foods cannot replace all the nutrients lost in processing. That is why nutritionists recommend eating whole-grain products and unprocessed foods whenever possible, according to the Food Guide Pyramid.

How foods are prepared affects their nutrient value, too. For example, boiling or cooking for a long time decreases the nutrient value of vegetables. They are most nutritious if baked, quickly steamed, or eaten raw. Adding sugars or fats also reduces the nutrient value of foods. Fried foods, for instance, including vegetables and meats, have reduced nutrient value because of the fat added in frying. Canned or frozen fruits and vegetables are lower in nutrient value if sugars have been added in their preparation.

What Are Calories?

Energy from foods is measured in units called calories. A calorie is the amount of energy required to raise the temperature of 1 gram of water 1 degree centigrade. The calories used to measure food energy are technically kilocalories (or 1000 calories). All foods supply calories, but some, such as fats and sugars, supply calories but few nutrients. That is why these foods are said to supply "empty calories." Different people need different amounts of calories each day for basic health (see chart below). To maintain a healthy weight, people must balance their calorie intake with the amount of calories their bodies use. Physical activity is an important way to use calories.

Recommended Daily Calorie Intake

For many sedentary women and some older adults	1600
For most children, active women, teenage girls, and many sedentary men	2200
For many active men, some very active women, and teenage boys	2800

Section D
HOW TO READ FOOD LABELS

Food labels list the ingredients contained in the foods we buy and provide information about their nutritional value. The main parts of food labels are the ingredients lists, the nutrition labels, and health claims. All packaged and processed foods (except fresh produce, meats, eggs, and milk) in the U.S. are required to have ingredients lists and specific nutrition information labels. Many other terms on labels, such as "fat-free" and "healthy," are also regulated by the government so that their meaning is the same for all foods.

Ingredients List

All foods containing more than one ingredient must have a list of ingredients on their labels. Ingredients must be listed in order by weight with the ingredient that is included in the greatest amount listed first. Reading the ingredients list is a good way to get a quick idea of the nutritional value of a food product—if sugar is listed first, for example, or occurs more than once on the list, you can assume the food's value is mainly as a sweet.

Nutrition Labels

The government now requires nutrition labels to help consumers be able to choose more healthful diets and to encourage food companies to provide more healthful foods. On page 110 is a sample of a standard nutrition label.

Health Claims

The Food and Drug Administration (FDA) has recently allowed food labels to carry information about the link between certain nutrients and specific diseases. For such a health claim to be made on a package, the FDA must determine that the link between the nutrient and the disease is supported by scientific evidence. Here is an example of a health claim that is allowed on a package of plain frozen vegetables: "While many factors affect heart disease, diets low in saturated fat and cholesterol may reduce the risk of this disease."

Labeling Terms

Many terms used on food labels to describe the nutritional value of foods are regulated by the government so that their meaning is the same from one product to another. However, a label may highlight a healthy feature of a product without highlighting less healthy features. For instance, a label might highlight the fact that the product is "100% Natural" or "Low-fat" but the main ingredient could be sugar. Reading the ingredients lists and the nutrition labels are better tools to help you get the nutritional benefits you want from your diet.

Here are some labeling terms and their meanings:

- "Free," as in "fat-free" or "sugar-free," means the food contains an insignificant amount of that nutrient (less than 0.5g of fat per serving, for example).

108 Environmental ACTION Food Teacher Resource Guide

- "Fresh" means the food is raw or unprocessed, has never been frozen or heated, and contains no preservatives.
- "Healthy" means the food is low in fat and saturated fat and contains only a small amount of cholesterol and sodium.
- "High, " as in "high fiber," means the food contains 20 percent or more of the Daily Value for the particular nutrient per serving.
- "Lean" is used for meat, poultry, and seafood and means it contains less than 10g of fat, less than 4.5g of saturated fat, and less than 95mg of cholesterol per serving.
- "Light" or "Lite" means either that the product has been altered to contain one-third fewer calories or one-half the fat or sodium of the regular product.
- "Natural" means the food contains no artificial colors or flavors or any synthetic ingredients. It does not necessarily mean it is grown naturally or organically or that it is a nutritionally valuable food. Many types of granola cereals are a good example of foods with labels highlighting that they are "natural," but they may be very high in saturated fat and sugar.
- "Source of," as in "Good Source of Vitamin C," means the food has 10 to 19 percent of the Daily Value of the named nutrient per serving.

Serving Size
The serving size reflects the amount usually eaten as one portion

List of Nutrients
The list of nutrients cover those most important to the health of Americans today. Nutrients are measured in grams (g) or milligrams (mg).

Calories per Gram
Larger packages may include information about calories per gram at the bottom of the label. It is general information that applies to all foods. It shows that 1 gram of fat provides about 9 calories; 1 gram of carbohydrate or protein provides about 4 calories.

Nutrition Facts

Serving Size 1/2 cup (114g)
Serving Per Container 4

Amount Per Serving

Calories 90   Calories from fat 30

	% Daily Value*
Total Fat 3g	5%
Saturated Fat 0g	0%
Cholesterol 0g	0%
Sodium 300mg	13%
Total Carbohydrate 13g	4%
Dietary Fiber 3g	12%
Sugars 3g	
Protein 3g	

Vitamin A 80%	•	Vitamin C 60%
Calcium 4%	•	Iron 4%

* Percent Daily Values are based on a 2,000-calorie diet. Your daily values may be higher or lower depending on your calorie needs:

	Calories	2,000	2,500
Total Fat	Less than	65g	80g
Sat Fat	Less than	20g	25g
Cholesterol	Less than	300mg	300mg
Sodium	Less than	2,400mg	2,400mg
Total Carbohydrate		300g	375g
Dietary Fiber		25g	30g

Calories per gram:
Fat 9 • Carbohydrate 4 • Protein 4

Source: Food and Drug Administration

Calories from Fat
Calories from fat are shown to help people limit the amount of fat in their diet. Dietary guidelines recommend that no more than 30 percent of daily calories comes from fat. To figure the percent of calories from fat for an individual product, divide the listed calories from fat by the total calories (listed to the left of calories from fat). In this case, 33 percent of the calories from this food are from fat (30 divided by 90 = .33 or 33 percent).

% Daily Value
% Daily Value shows the percent of the recommended daily amount of the nutrient that is contained in one serving of this food. You can use the % Daily Value as a quick guideline to get a general idea of how a serving of this food fits into the total daily diet. For nutrients related to health problems (such as fat and cholesterol), the goal is to eat 100 percent or less of the Daily Value each day. A good rule of thumb is if the % Daily Value is 5% or less, the food contributes a small amount of that nutrient. For nutrients that are needed in greater quantity (such as calcium or fiber), the goal is to eat at least 100 percent of the Daily Value each day.

Daily Value
The Daily Value must be listed on larger packages. It is the total number of the nutrients that people should eat each day for a healthy diet. Values are given for a diet of 2000 and 2500 calories. Values for fats, cholesterol, and sodium are maximum amounts (for instance, less than 65g of fat should be included in a 2000-calorie diet). Values for carbohydrates and fiber are minimum amounts (for instance, 300g or more of carbohydrates should be included in a 2000-calorie diet).

Section E
KNOWING WHAT IS GOOD FOR YOU

Fat, sugar, cholesterol, sodium, and fiber are the nutrients most Americans need to adjust in their diets. The tendency is to get too little fiber and too much fat, sugar, cholesterol, and sodium. A lot of favorite snack foods—potato chips, French fries, sodas, fast-food burgers, cookies—have high levels of sugar, salt, and fat but low levels of vitamins and minerals. That's why they are called "junk foods." Eating a healthy diet doesn't mean giving up these foods altogether: Be selective; eat a balanced diet that limits fat, sugar, cholesterol, and sodium overall; and get enough fiber.

People often think that avoiding fat and sugars will correct weight problems But neither "fat-free" nor "sugar-free" mean "calorie-free." Generally to reduce weight, eat a healthy diet of a variety of foods, reduce the total amount of calories, and increase physical activity. Often, increasing physical activity is all that is needed. People who are concerned about their weight should talk to a health professional before making diet changes.

Fats

A certain amount of fat is necessary for health, but the link between excess dietary fat and heart disease, cancer, and weight problems makes it important to limit the amount of fat in the diet. The Dietary Guidelines recommend that fat intake be limited to 30 percent or less of our daily calories. In a 1600-calorie diet, 30 percent of calories amounts to 53 grams of fat; in a 2200-calorie diet, it's 73 grams of fat; and in a 2800-calorie diet, it's 93 grams of fat (you can calculate these figures yourself if you know that each gram of fat provides 9 calories). Saturated fats should be limited to less than 10 percent of daily calories.

About half of the daily level of fat is present in the foods we eat, without any added fat and even choosing the lowest fat choices. In general, plant foods are lower in fats than foods that come from animals (meats and dairy products), but many lean meats and low-fat or nonfat dairy products are available. Also, many popular ways of preparing vegetables and grains make them high-fat choices (such as fried vegetables, vegetables and breads with butter, doughnuts, croissants).

Here are some tips for reducing dietary fat:

- Read nutrition labels and check the amounts and kinds of fat.
- Choose low-fat and nonfat foods from the five main food groups.
- Be sparing with fats added when cooking or at the table—oils, butter, margarine, mayonnaise, gravy, salad dressing.
- Use unsaturated vegetables oils and margarines that list a liquid vegetable oil as the first ingredient on the label (solid margarines are higher in saturated fats).
- Limit products high in saturated fats such as nondairy creamers, baked goods (pie crusts, cakes, cookies), popcorn popped in coconut oil, products made with palm oil, chocolate, and high-fat animal products.
- Choose meats labeled "lean" or "extra lean." Trim fat from meat; take the skin off poultry. Limit intake of high-fat processed meats such as sausages, salami, and other cold cuts.
- Use egg yolks and organ meats (such as liver) sparingly.
- Choose lean fish and beans as low-fat sources of protein instead of higher fat meats or dairy products.

Sugars

The main problem with sweets is that they are a source of calories but provide very limited nutrients. People tend to eat them in place of more nutritious foods—drinking sodas instead of milk or juice, eating candy instead of fruits or vegetables. Too many sweets can also contribute to tooth decay. Limiting sugars in the diet is important for people who have low calorie needs. For very active people with high calorie needs, sugar can be an added source of energy.

Many foods naturally contain sugars—fruits and milk, for example. It is sugars that are added to foods that provide extra calories without vitamins or minerals. Added sugars are found in foods such as candies, jams, ice cream, fruits canned in syrup, and sweet bakery goods. Added sugars have many different forms and names. The list below shows some of the sugars you may find listed in the ingredients lists of different foods.

Terms for Sugars in Foods

brown sugar	lactose
corn sweetener	levulose
corn syrup	maltose
dextrose	molasses
dried fruit	raw sugar
fructose	sorbitol
fruit juice concentrate	sucrose
glucose	sugar
high-fructose corn syrup	syrup
honey	xylitol
invert sugar	

Foods and Added Sugars*

Food Group	Added Sugars (teaspoons)
Bread Group	
Muffin, 1 medium	1
Cookies, 2 medium	1
Doughnut, 1 medium	2
Cake, frosted, $\frac{1}{16}$ average	6
Fruit pie, 2 crust, $\frac{1}{6}$ 8-inch pie	6
Fruit Group	
Fruit, canned in juice, $\frac{1}{2}$ cup	0
Fruit, canned in light syrup, $\frac{1}{2}$ cup	2
Fruit, canned in heavy syrup, $\frac{1}{2}$ cup	4
Milk Group	
Milk, plain, 1 cup	0
Chocolate milk, 2%, 1 cup	3
Lowfat yogurt, plain, 8 oz	0
Lowfat yogurt, flavored, 8 oz	5
Lowfat yogurt, fruit, 8 oz	7
Ice cream or frozen yogurt, $\frac{1}{2}$ cup	3
Chocolate shake, 10 fl. oz	9
Other	
Sugar, jam, jelly, 1 tsp	1
Chocolate bar, 1 oz	3
Sherbet, $\frac{1}{2}$ cup	5
Cola, 12 fl. oz	9
Fruit drink, lemonade, 12 fl. oz	12

*Check product labels.

If one of these sugars is listed first or second, or if several of them appear on a food label, the food is high in sugar.

The Dietary Guidelines suggest that we avoid getting too many calories from sugars by limiting added sugars on average to 6 teaspoons a day in a 1600-calorie diet, 12 teaspoons a day in a 2200-calorie diet, and 18 teaspoons in a 2800-calorie diet. For comparing these suggestions to information on food labels, it is helpful to know that 1 teaspoon sugar = 4 grams. The chart on page 108 gives you an idea of the number of teaspoons of added sugars in some different foods.

Cholesterol

Cholesterol is a fat-like substance manufactured by the liver. It is used to build tissues and cell membranes and to produce certain hormones that are needed to regulate the body. Our bodies make all the cholesterol we need—we do not need to get any from our diets. Cholesterol that we eat raises the level of cholesterol in our blood and increases the risk for heart disease.

The typical American diet contains quite a bit of cholesterol. Cholesterol is found only in foods that come from animals; plant foods do not contain cholesterol. Foods high in cholesterol are meats (especially organ meats such as liver), poultry, fish, egg yolks, and higher fat dairy products. Lower fat products contain less cholesterol than high-fat products. The recommended limit for cholesterol per day is 300mg. One egg yolk contains 213mg, a 3-ounce piece of liver contains 331mg, one cup of whole milk contains 33mg. As the Food Guide Pyramid suggests, cholesterol can be limited by using lower fat products; eating dry beans and peas sometimes instead of meat; avoiding foods high in cholesterol; and eating more grains, fruits, and vegetables.

Sodium

Sodium is a mineral that is essential for almost every function of the human body. Although the words "salt" and "sodium" are often used to mean the same thing, salt is actually only one form of sodium. Salt and sodium occur naturally in many different foods such as milk, meats, baking soda, and some vegetables. Salt is added in many foods from bread to canned and frozen products to add flavor and act as a preservative.

Although sodium is essential in the body, in some people high sodium intake is associated with high blood pressure. Health authorities suggest that the intake of sodium be limited to 2400mg per day. Most of the sodium and salt we eat is added while cooking, added at the table, or found in processed and prepared foods. To eat less sodium:

- Read nutrition labels and choose foods with a low sodium content.
- Use less salt in cooking and at the table (the preference for salt weakens as less is used).
- Go easy on foods high in sodium including cured meats, luncheon meats, cheeses, soy sauce and many other sauces, pickles, and many canned foods including soups and vegetables.
- Choose lower-salt and no-salt varieties of snack foods, salad dressings, and other products.

The chart on page 114 will give you an idea of the amount of sodium found in different foods.

Sodium in Foods*

	Sodium (mg)
Salt, 1 Tbs	2000
Soy sauce, 1 Tbs	1030
Ham, lean, roasted, 3 oz	1020
Dill pickle, 1 medium	930
Vegetable soup, canned, 1 cup	820
Process cheeses, 2 oz	800
Tomato juice, canned, $\frac{3}{4}$ cup	660
Bologna, 2 oz	580
Vegetables, canned or frozen with sauce, $\frac{1}{2}$ cup	140–460
Natural cheeses, $1\frac{1}{2}$ oz	110–450
Tuna, canned in water, 3 oz	300
Corn chips, salted, 1 oz	235
Ketchup, mustard, steak sauce, 1 Tbs	130–230
Salad dressing, 1 Tbs	75–220
Potato chips, salted, 1 oz	130
Peanuts, roasted in oil, salted, 1 oz	120

*Check product labels.

Fiber

Fiber is essential to digestion and may reduce the risk of heart disease and some cancers. Fiber is found only in plant foods, particularly whole-grain breads and cereals, dried beans and peas, vegetables, and fruits.

Whole grains, unlike grains that have been refined (such as white rice or foods made with white flour), are rich sources of fiber and other important nutrients. To be sure you are eating foods with a significant amount of whole grains, look for the words "whole" or "whole-grain" or "whole-wheat" to be among the first ingredients on the ingredients list (not just highlighted in the product name or on the label). Brown rice is the only whole-grain rice. Many breakfast cereals and breads are good sources of whole grains if whole-grain ingredients are used in the greater quantity than other ingredients.

Section F
WHAT YOU CAN DO: MAKING FOOD CHOICES THAT ARE HEALTHY FOR THE ENVIRONMENT

We can choose foods and encourage food production practices that are healthy both for our bodies and for the environment. Below are some examples of actions that can be taken and some suggestions for school lunch programs based on what some schools have done already.

What You Can Do

- Eat lower on the food chain (eat fewer animal products and more grains, fruits, and vegetables).
- Minimize your intake of fats and chemical additives.
- Purchase or grow your own organic food products to reduce the use of chemical pesticides and fertilizers; grow an organic garden on your school campus!
- Choose whole-grain, unprocessed foods to reduce the use of energy and to promote better health.
- Purchase and eat locally grown or locally produced food products to reduce both energy and transportation costs.
- To reduce packaging waste, avoid over-packaged food products and choose packaging that can be recycled or reused. When possible, buy foods in bulk.
- Reuse and/or recycle food packaging waste.
- Promote a "zero-waste-lunch" program at school. Encourage students to bring their lunches in reusable cloth bags with reusable plastic containers and cloth napkins.
- Educate students, faculty, administrators, and parent groups through discussions, letters, posters, assemblies, and the school paper.
- Set special days at the school to highlight cultural foods, nutrition, and taste testing of new food dishes.

Some Ideas for School Lunch Programs

Your school lunch providers are probably one of your best resources for learning more about nutrition and preparing healthy foods. Here are some ideas that have been used in some schools to provide healthy lunches that also help the environment.

- Use produce grown by students in an organic garden on campus.
- Add a salad bar. Include cooked beans, sprouts, and seeds along with a variety of vegetables. Offer low-fat or fat-free dressings.
- Offer vegetarian soups, pastas, pizza, tacos, lasagna.
- Offer low-fat, meatless burgers or hot dogs.
- Offer pastries, rolls, cookies and other baked goods that are whole-grain and made with vegetable fat or no fat.
- Use vegetable oil for frying and sautéing instead of animal fat.
- Offer vegetarian baked beans instead of pork and beans, chili beans instead of chili con carne.
- Offer fresh fruits and vegetables instead of sugary or salty canned fruits or vegetables.

GLOSSARY

amino acids the building blocks that go together to build proteins

calorie a measure of energy available in food

carbohydrates nutrients that are the main source of energy for living things

cholesterol a fatty substance found in blood that is important in metabolism

drought a long period of no rainfall

fortified enriched with vitamins and minerals

glucose a type of sugar

metabolism all of the chemical processes that occur in an organism

mineral an element that helps the body to function normally and to use other nutrients

nutrient any substance that the body needs to live and grow

overgrazing process of allowing livestock to eat grasses down to the roots, thereby leaving the topsoil vulnerable to erosion

proteins nutrients that provide the body with materials for cell growth and repair and control body functions

saturated fat a solid or semisolid animal fat, such as butter

sodium a metallic element that reacts with water; occurs in nature combined with other elements: sodium bicarbonate (baking soda), sodium carbonate (soaps), sodium chloride (table salt)

soil depletion process of overfarming, overgrazing, overuse of pesticides and herbicides by which the soil is stripped of nutrients

starch a substance found in plants that is important to metabolism

sugars a group of soluble, sweet-tasting carbohydrates; sucrose; sugars include glucose, lactose, maltose, fructose.

vitamin an organic substance that helps to control the body's chemical functions

Teacher Resources

ORGANIZATIONS

American Dietetic Association/National Center for Nutrition and Dietetics Consumer Nutrition Hotline

216 W. Jackson Boulevard
Chicago, IL 60606
Phone: (312) 899-0040
Hotline: (800) 366-1655
Internet: http://www.eatright.org

Center for Science in the Public Interest (CSPI)

1875 Connecticut Avenue, NW, Suite 300
Washington, DC 20009
(202) 332-9110
Fax: (202) 265-4954

CSPI is a consumer advocacy organization whose twin missions are to conduct innovative research and advocacy programs in health and nutrition and to provide consumers with current, useful information about their own health and well-being. CSPI conducts research on nutrition, food safety, alcohol, health, the environment, and other issues.

Products and Services: *Safe Food: Eating Wisely in a Risky World; Nutrition Action Healthletter; Quick and Healthy Low-fat Cooking;* Chemical Cuisine posters and software program; information about dozens of the most common food additives; The Healthy Eating Pyramid three-dimensional mobile.

Community Nutrition Institute

910 17th Street, NW, Suite 413
Washington DC 20006
(202) 776-0595
Fax: (202) 776-0595
E-mail: cnii@igc.apc.org

CNI is a nonprofit consumer interest group that functions as a public advocate for safe food and health policies. The institute provides policy analysis and consumer information and education.

Products and Services: *Nutrition Week,* an eight-page weekly covering legislation, regulations, and other relevant developments concerning food stamps, child nutrition programs, WIC, and nutrition programs for the elderly. The newsletter also addresses a wide range of consumer issues, including food prices, safety, and quality; initiatives to improve the USDA and its sub-agencies; and federal trade and environmental policies.

EarthSave Foundation

706 Fredrick Street
Santa Cruz, CA 95060-2205
(408) 423-4069
Fax: (408) 458-0255
To order publications call: (800) 362-3648
E-mail: earthsave@aol.com

EarthSave is a nonprofit organization that educates people about the powerful effects their food choices have on the environment and their health. EarthSave was founded in 1988 by John Robbins, author of *Diet for a New America,* and advocates sustainable agriculture, conservation of resources, and sound nutrition through a low-fat, organic, plant-based diet.

Products and Services: *The EarthSave Catalog,* including the *Healthy School Lunch Action Guide;* the Healthy School Lunch Program Video, which is a four-minute video about the impact of the Healthy School Lunch Program; *Choices for Our Future,* an introduction for people of any age who want to learn the environmental basics; *Diet for a New America,* which addresses the major health, environmental, and compassionate reasons for individuals to reduce their consumption of meat, poultry, and dairy food; *May All Be Fed:* discloses the commercially motivated programming that has shaped and continues to shape much of the prevailing food consciousness in our society; *Nutrition, Health & Recipes;* vegan cookbooks.

The Feingold Association of the United States

P.O. Box 6550
Alexandria, VA 22306
(703) 768-FAUS

FAUS is a nonprofit volunteer organization whose main purpose is to help those who wish to improve their children's behavior or their own health by changing their diet. The Feingold Program was developed at the Kaiser-Permanente Medical Center in San Francisco. It is a nutritious, risk-free diet that eliminates synthetic food colorings and flavors, three antioxidant preservatives—BHA, BHT, and TBHQ—and natural salicylates.

Products and Services: Foodlist, a book containing the name brand products that have been researched and are recommended; *The Feingold Handbook,* which provides a step-by-step guide for successfully using the Program; *Pure Facts; Why Your Child Is Hyperactive; The Feingold Cookbook.*

Food & Water Incorporated

Depot Hill Road
RR1, Box 114
Marshfield, VT 05658-9702
(802) 426-3700
Fax: (802) 426-3711

A national grassroots organization of people concerned about their health and the quality of their food and environment. Their goal is to prevent technologies that threaten the safety of the food supply, such as food irradiation, cancer-causing pesticides, and the genetically engineered bovine growth hormone—rBGH.

Products and Services: For a $25 membership one receives Action Alerts, issue updates, and their quarterly newsletter, *Safe Food News.*

Foodservice & Packaging Institute, Inc.

1901 North Moore Street, Suite 1111
Arlington, VA 22209
(703) 527-7505
Fax: (703) 527-7512
(800) TIPS-FPI for a free FPI information kit

A nonprofit trade association for manufacturers, raw material suppliers, machinery suppliers, and distributors of foodservice disposable products, such as single-use cups, plates, cutlery, trays, and other paper, plastic, and aluminum items.

Products and Services: "Foodservice Disposables: Should I Feel Guilty?" is a video package to help students explore environmental issues surrounding foodservice disposables. The 11½-minute video, companion booklet, and teacher's discussion brochure address issues such as recycling, solid waste disposal, resource conservation, and ozone-layer protection. This package is appropriate for grades 6–12 and is available free of charge.

The Humane Farming Association

1550 California Street, Suite 6
San Francisco, CA 94109
(650) 771-2253

The association is dedicated to stopping the abuse of farm animals and ensuring healthful, drug-free food.

Products and Services: Pamphlets, including *Bovine Growth Hormone; A Look Inside the Pork Industry; The Dangers of Factory Farming; Milk-Fed Veal;* and *Anything Goes With Eggs.*

Humane Society of the United States

Eating with Conscience Campaign
2100 L Street, NW
Washington, DC 20037
(301) 258-3054
(301) 258-3081

Provides guidelines on how to choose a diet of compassion and concern for your health and the health of the planet. The Eating with Conscience Campaign is designed to educate people about sustainable agriculture and the dangers of current methods of food production.

Institute for Food and Development Policy

398 60th Street
Oakland, CA 94618
Phone: (510) 654-4400
Fax: (510) 654-4551
E-mail: foodfirst@lgc.apc.org
Internet:
http://www.netspace.org/hungerweb/FoodFirst/index.htm

Research and education organization. High school and grade school curricula available on issues of food production, world hunger, and the environment. Free catalog available.

Mothers and Others for a Livable Planet

40 W. 20th Street
New York, NY 10011
(212) 242-0010
Fax: (212) 242-0545

A national nonprofit advocacy group dedicated to bringing everyday environmentalism into homes and communities by providing information that is accessible and practical. M&O informs consumers and mobilizes consumers to demand healthy choices in their supermarkets.

Products and Services: *The Way We Grow: Good-Sense Solutions for Protecting Our Families from Pesticides in Food;* Shoppers' Campaign Kit, with information for persuading your supermarket to stock organic foods; *Organics in the Supermarket,* a shoppers' guide to supermarkets around the country that are the best suppliers of organic foods; *Organic Marketplace,* a mail-order catalog of over 40 popular organic foods (free); *Mothers' Milk List* of brand names, supermarkets, dairies, and distributors that offer dairy products from cows that have not been treated with synthetic bovine growth hormone.

National Cattlemen's Association and Beef Board

Communications Department
P.O. Box 3469
Englewood, CO 80155
(303) 694-0305
Fax: (303) 694-2851

The association represents cattlemen and the beef industry, providing a catalog of educational materials. Many of these materials are either free or offered at a nominal charge.

Organic Trade Association

P.O. Box 1078
Greenfield, MA 01302
Phone: (413) 774-7511
Fax: (413) 774-6432
E-mail: ota@igc.apc.org

Physicians Committee For Responsible Medicine

5100 Wisconsin Avenue, Suite 404
Washington, DC 20016
(202) 686-2210
Fax: (202) 686-2216

A nonprofit organization of physicians and lay people to promote nutrition, preventive medicine, ethical research practices, and compassionate medical policy. PCRM proposes a federal nutrition policy called The New Four Food Groups that puts a priority on health. The program includes an effective nutrition curriculum for schools.

Products and Services: Quarterly newsletter, *Good Medicine,* and numerous fact sheets, booklets, audio tapes, posters, and books on nutrition and research issues.

Public Voice for Food and Health Policy

1101 14th Street, NW, Suite 710
Washington DC 20005
(202) 371-1840
Fax: (202) 371-1910

A national nonprofit research, education, and advocacy organization that promotes a safer, healthier, and more affordable food supply for all Americans. Their work is organized around four major program areas: agriculture and the environment; food safety; nutrition and healthy eating; and access to affordable food. Publications address commodity policy, food safety policy, food labeling, nutrition education, school lunch, and sustainable agriculture and pesticide policy.

Pure Food Campaign

1660 L Street, NW, Suite 216
Washington DC 20036
(800) 253-0681
(202) 775-1132
Fax: (218)226-4164
E-mail: purefood@aol.com

Pure Food is a project of the Foundation on Economic Trends, whose activities are centered around the environmental, economic, and ethical concerns raised by the development and commercialization of emerging technologies, specifically biotechnology. Through education, litigation, and grass-roots organizing, Pure Food is working to promote sustainable agriculture and a healthy food chain.

Vegetarian Education Network

P.O. Box 339
Oxford PA, 19363
(717) 529-8638
Fax (717) 529-3000
E-mail: howonearth@aol.com

A nonprofit research and education project devoted to promoting the vegetarian perspective in schools through education and school lunches and supporting young vegetarians and advocating compassionate, ecologically sound living. They provide information on how to make changes at the school as well as other educational information.

Products and Services: *How On Earth!* a quarterly newsletter for and by teenagers.

The Vegetarian Resource Group

P.O. Box 1463
Baltimore, MD 21203
(410) 366-VEGE
Internet: http://envirolink.org/arrs/VR-G/home.html

A nonprofit organization dedicated to educating the public on vegetarianism and the interrelated issues of health, nutrition, ecology, ethics, and world hunger. Their health professionals, activists, and educators will work with businesses and individuals to bring about healthy changes in the school, workplace, and community. Registered dieticians and physicians aid in the development of nutrition-related publications and answer member or media questions about the vegetarian diet. Publications include brochures, recipe books, pamphlets, article reprints, and the *Vegetarian Journal.*

GOVERNMENT AGENCIES

U.S. Department of Agriculture

Fourteen and Independent Avenue, SW
Washington, DC 20250
(202) 720-8732
General Information: (202) 720-2791

Products and Services: a directory listing sources of information in the U.S. Department of Agriculture and its various agencies, such as the school lunch and breakfast programs. It also includes names of the various Freedom of Information Act officers. Note particularly the following publications:

The Food Guide Pyramid, HG-252
Nutrition and Your Health: Dietary Guidelines for Americans, HG-232
Dietary Guidelines and Your Diet, HG-232-1 through 7
Preparing Foods and Planning Menus, HG-232-8
Making Bag Lunches, Snacks and Desserts, HG-232-9
Shopping for Food and Making Meals in Minutes, HG-232-10
Eating Better When Eating Out, HG-232-11

USDA Center for Nutrition Policy and Promotion

1120 20th Street, NW
Suite 200, North Lobby
Washington, DC 20036

BOOKS AND PAMPHLETS

The A to Z Guide To Toxic Foods And How To Avoid Them

Lynn Sonberg
New York: Simon & Schuster Inc., 1992

Nearly 300 complete, up-to-date entries on contaminants, pesticides, and other pollutants. This alphabetized guide will tell you which foods are relatively free of pesticides and other contaminants and which should be used with caution, especially by children; how to buy, clean, cook, and store each listed food to insure maximum healthfulness; which growers and supermarkets sell meats, fruits, and vegetables free of hormones and pesticides; how to evaluate processed foods for contaminants. 258 pages.
$5.99

A Consumer's Dictionary of Food Additives

Ruth Winter
New York: Crown Publishers, 1994

Definitions written for the layman, covering harmful and desirable ingredients found in packaged foods. 425 pages.
$14

Diet for a New America

John Robbins
Stillpoint Publishing, 1987

Diet for a Poisoned Planet: How to Choose Safe Foods for You and Your Family

David Steinman
New York: Ballantine, 1990

A guide to selecting, preparing, and serving the most-life-enhancing foods available in any supermarket today. Hundreds of foods are reviewed and rated, along with information on which brands are best, which companies and agricultural regions produce the safest foods, and tips on how to prepare foods that are more healthful. Includes an appendix listing national and local resources with products and information. 392 pages.
$12.50

Diet for a Small Planet, Tenth Anniversary Edition

Frances Moore Lappé
New York: Ballantine Books/Random House, 1982

The Gaia Atlas of Planet Management

Norman Myers, ed.
Pan Books, 1985

The Global Ecology Handbook

Walter H. Corson, ed.
Beacon Press, 1990

Healthy School Lunch Action Guide

Susan Campbell and Todd Winant
Santa Cruz, CA: EarthSave Foundation, 1994

This comprehensive step-by-step Action Guide contains information on teaching children what is in their food, where it comes from, and how to make healthy food choices; how to approach the school district, foodservice personnel, teachers, and parents; teaching aids, lesson plans, sample letters; food service resources; low-fat vegetarian recipes; and classroom handouts with nutritional and environmental facts.

Keeping Food Fresh: How to Choose and Store Everything You Eat

Janet Bailey
New York: Harper & Row, 1989

A field guide to shopping, an encyclopedia of information on storing foods, an emergency

manual on how to identify what has gone bad, and a consumer guide on storage equipment. 391 pages.
$12

The National Audubon Society Almanac of the Environment

Valerie Harms, ed.
New York: G.P.Putnam's Sons, 1994

Old MacDonald's Factory Farm

C. David Coats
New York: Continuum Publishing Company, 1991

The subtitle—*The Myth of the Traditional Farm and The Shocking Truth About Animal Suffering in Today's Agribusiness*—sums up the content and perspective of this book. 188 pages.
$11.95

Organizing for Better School Food

CSPI's Children Nutrition Project
Washington, DC: Center For Science in the Public Interest, 1991.

A comprehensive plan of action for parents, activists, and food-service directors who are committed to improving school nutrition.
$7

Pesticide Perspective: Pesticides in Food

Santa Cruz, CA: Agroecology Program, UCSC, 1990

Addresses concerns about pesticide regulation, reduction of exposure to pesticide residue, interpretation of food labels and claims, and other issues.
Free from the publisher.

The Power of Your Plate

A Plan for Better Living
Neal D. Barnard, M.D.
Summertown, TN: Book Publishing Co., 1990

Seventeen experts discuss how our eating habits have evolved and determine our chances for a long and healthy life. Available from Physicians Committee for Responsible Medicine. 238 pages.
$10.95

Safe Food: Eating Wisely in a Risky World

Michael F. Jacobson, Ph.D.; Lisa Y. Lefferts, M.S.; and Anne Witte Garland.
Washington, DC: Center for Science in the Public Interest, 1991.

This book describes which foods are most likely to contain pesticides, salmonella, antibiotics, and food additives.

The Way We Grow

by Anne Witte Garland with Mothers & Others for a Livable Planet
Berkeley Books, 1993

Sub-titled *Good-Sense Solutions for Protecting Our Families from Pesticides in Food*. Addresses what is wrong with the way our food is grown, sustainable agriculture, actions one can take, and tools for organizing. 90 pages.

The Wax Cover-Up: What Consumers Aren't Told About Coatings and Pesticides on Fresh Produce

Washington, DC: Center for Science in the Public Interest, 1991.

Gives background information and suggestions on how to get your supermarket to obey the wax-disclosure law.

MAGAZINES AND NEWSLETTERS

Consumer Reports

Consumer Union
101 Truman Avenue
Yonkers, NY 10703
$20/year

Nutrition Action Health Letter

Center for Science in the Public Interest
1875 Connecticut Avenue, NW, Suite 300
Washington, DC 20009-5728
(800) 237-4874
$24/ten issues per year

Organic Gardening

Rodale Press
33 East Minor Street
Emmaus, PA 18098

Vegetarian Times

P.O. Box 446
Mt. Morris, IL 61054-8081

PRODUCTS AND SERVICES

National Organic Directory

Community Alliance with Family Farmers
P.O. Box 464
Davis, CA 95617
(916) 756-8518
Fax: (916) 756-7857
(800) 852-3832

A guide to organic information and resources. Lists farmers, wholesalers, farm suppliers, support businesses, certification groups. Provides general information on organic laws, marketing. Indexes of commodities bought and sold, support business services, and mail order to the general public.

The New Food Label: There's Something in It for Everybody

International Food Information Council Foundation
1100 Connecticut Avenue, NW, Suite 430
Washington, DC 20036

A 50-page food label education program for high school students, covering a range of food labeling topics. Includes five lesson plans with handouts, charts, worksheets, activities.
$5 per copy

Real Foodservices

William C. Stewart, President
1155 Juniper Avenue
Boulder, CO 80304
(800) 291-2302

Comprised of the leading manufacturers in the natural products industry, PRF provides one-stop shopping for vegetarian, whole food, and organic products for the food service buyer.

Blackline Masters

Name

ACTIVITY SHEET 1 EXPLORE

FOOD PRODUCTION AND THE ENVIRONMENT (part 1)

In response to a growing world population and a growing demand in developed countries for meat, eggs, and dairy products, methods have been developed to increase food production. Although these methods do increase food production, concerns have been raised because of the environmental problems that may result.

1. Some modern food production practices are shown in the chart below, followed by a list of environmental problems. Work together with a partner to identify how environmental problems may be linked to food production practices. In each box of the chart, write the number of the environmental problems that may arise. There may be more than one problem linked to a food production practice.

 Food Production Practices.

Pack foods in excessive packaging for sale in stores.	Clear land of trees to create range land and crop land.	Fatten livestock by feeding them grains and soybeans grown with the help of chemical fertilizers and pesticides.
Use fertilizers made from synthetic chemicals to increase crop yields.	Raise large numbers of livestock for human consumption, which includes growing grain for feed.	Graze livestock on open ranges where they can eat grasses down to the roots.
Grow produce in large quantity in special regions, transport it to a distribution center, and then transport it to the point where it's sold.	Use pesticides to kill pests and produce more attractive and more abundant crops.	Grow large quantities of a single crop year after year.

Investigate Foods and the Environment 131

ACTIVITY SHEET

Name _____

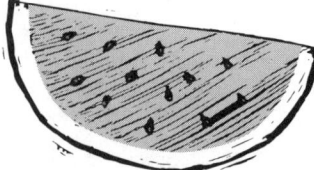

FOOD PRODUCTION AND THE ENVIRONMENT (part 2)

Environmental Problems

1. Pollution of water, air, and land
2. Use of fossil fuels (gas, oil, coal)
3. Use of fresh water
4. Destruction of natural habitats
5. Erosion of topsoil
6. Depletion of topsoil
7. Increase in waste that will need to be disposed of

2. Choose two of the food production practices and explain the possible impact they have on the environment.

_____
_____
_____
_____
_____
_____
_____

3. On a separate sheet of paper, identify some actions you, your family, your school, or your community might take to help reduce or solve the problems caused by each of the food production practices shown in the table.

ACTIVITY SHEET

Name _____

THE FOOD GUIDE PYRAMID (part 1)

Complete the drawing of the Food Guide Pyramid, including the names of the basic foods in each of the food groups. Fill in the recommended servings per day according to your needs as shown in the chart below. You may want to draw pictures of some of the food items in each group.

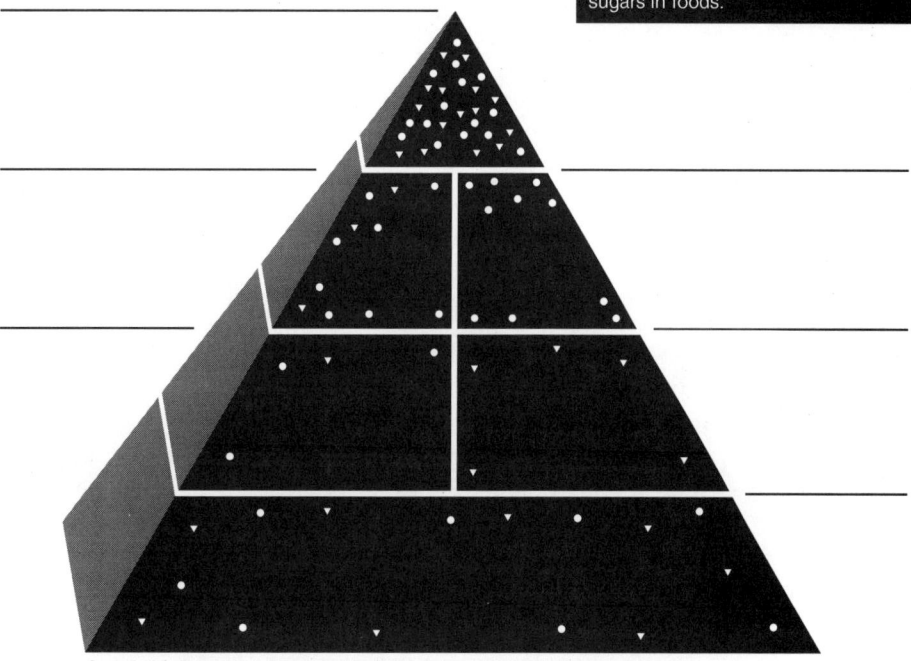

The Food Guide Pyramid
A Guide to Daily Food Choices

KEY
● Fat (naturally occurring and added)
▼ Sugars (added)

These symbols show fat and added sugars in foods.

Source: U.S. Department of Agriculture/U.S. Department of Health and Human Services

Recommended Daily Servings

Food Group	For Teenage Boys*	For Teenage Girls**	For All Ages
Bread	11	9	6–11
Vegetable	5	4	3–5
Fruit	4	3	2–4
Milk	3	3	2–3
Meat	2–3 (or 7 ounces)	2 (or 6 ounces)	2–3
Fats, sweets	Use sparingly	Use sparingly	Use sparingly

* and for active men and very active women   ** and for most children, active women, and sedentary men

Use the Food Guide Pyramid   133

ACTIVITY SHEET

Name

THE FOOD GUIDE PYRAMID (part 2)

Create a menu plan for one day that includes breakfast, lunch, dinner, and snacks and meets the requirements of the Food Guide Pyramid. Remember that fats, oils, and sweets are to be used sparingly. Use the chart below to create your menu and tally the servings for each food group.

Meal	Food Group	Number of Servings
BREAKFAST		
LUNCH		
DINNER		
SNACKS		

Use the Food Guide Pyramid

ACTIVITY SHEET

Name

FOOD LABELS (part 1)

Compare the three food labels shown below and use them to answer the questions in part 2.

Nutrition Facts		Wheat Squares Sweetened		Corn Flakes Not Sweetened		Mixed Grain Flakes Sweetened	
Serving Size 1 Box		(35g)		(19g)		(27g)	
Serving per container		1		1		1	
Amount Per Serving							
Calories 90		120		70		100	
Calories from fat		0		0		0	
			% Daily Value*		% Daily Value*		% Daily Value*
Total Fat		0g	0%	0g	0%	0g	0%
Saturated Fat		0g	0%	0g	0%	0g	0%
Cholesterol		0mg	0%	0mg	0%	0mg	0%
Sodium		0mg	0%	200mg	8%	120mg	5%
Potassium		125mg	4%	25mg	1%	30mg	1%
Total Carbohydrate		29g	10%	17g	6%	24g	8%
Dietary Fiber		3g	12%	1g	4%	1g	4%
Sugars		5g		6g		13g	
Protein		4g		1g		1g	

* Percent Daily Values are based on a 2,000-calorie diet. Your daily values may be higher or lower depending on your calorie needs:

	Calories	2,000	2,500
Total Fat	Less than	65g	80g
Sat Fat	Less than	20g	25g
Cholesterol	Less than	300mg	300mg
Sodium	Less than	2,400mg	2,400mg
Potassium	Less than	3,500mg	3,500mg
Total Carbohydrate		300g	375g
Dietary Fiber		25g	30g

Vitamin A	0%	10%	10%
Vitamin C	0%	15%	90%
Calcium	0%	0%	0%
Iron	10%	6%	20%
Thiamin	30%	15%	20%
Riboflavin	30%	15%	20%
Niacin	30%	15%	20%
Vitamin B₆	30%	15%	20%

Source: Food and Drug Administration

Evaluate Nutritional Values

ACTIVITY SHEET

Name _____

FOOD LABELS (part 2)

1. Which nutrients do the labels indicate are included in these cereals?
   _____
   _____
   _____
   _____

2. Which of these cereals would you choose if you were on a low-salt diet?
   _____
   _____

3. Which would you avoid if you were on a low-salt diet?
   _____

4. Which of these cereals would you choose if you wanted to lose weight, and why would you choose it?
   _____
   _____
   _____

5. What other information do you get from these labels to help you compare these cereals?
   _____
   _____
   _____
   _____
   _____
   _____
   _____
   _____

136   Evaluate Nutritional Values

ACTIVITY SHEET

Name _____

CHOOSING FOODS (part 1)

Use the following list of foods to create healthy and well-balanced breakfast, lunch, and dinner menus for at least three days. Use classroom resources, the Food Guide Pyramid, the nutrient chart, and Issues and Information as you work together in small groups.

- apple
- bagel and cream cheese
- baked beans
- banana
- beef stew
- bran muffin
- bread
- carrots
- cereal (corn flakes, raisin bran)
- cheese
- cheese omelet
- chicken
- chicken noodle soup
- cole slaw
- egg salad
- fruit salad
- green salad
- hamburger
- lentil soup
- macaroni salad
- meatballs
- milk
- noodles
- oatmeal
- orange
- orange juice
- pancakes
- pasta
- peanut butter and jelly
- pear
- pork
- potatoes
- potato salad
- power shake (yogurt, fruit, juice)
- rice
- stir-fry vegetables
- tacos
- tomatoes
- tomato soup
- tuna sandwich
- turkey club sandwich
- water
- yogurt

DAY 1

BREAKFAST	LUNCH	DINNER
_____	_____	_____
_____	_____	_____
_____	_____	_____
_____	_____	_____
_____	_____	_____
_____	_____	_____

DAY 2

BREAKFAST	LUNCH	LUNCH
_____	_____	_____
_____	_____	_____
_____	_____	_____
_____	_____	_____
_____	_____	_____
_____	_____	_____

ACTIVITY SHEET

Name _____

CHOOSING FOODS (Part 2)

DAY 3

BREAKFAST	LUNCH	DINNER
_____	_____	_____
_____	_____	_____
_____	_____	_____
_____	_____	_____
_____	_____	_____
_____	_____	_____

1. How does using the nutrient chart influence your choices? What other considerations are there?

    _____
    _____
    _____
    _____

2. How does food preparation relate to nutrition?

    _____
    _____
    _____
    _____

3. What foods would you add to the menus that are not on the list?

    _____
    _____
    _____
    _____

Practice Making Food Choices

ACTIVITY SHEET

Name _____

NOTES ON NUTRITION, DIET, AND HEALTH (part 1)

Use this sheet to record information you learn from the guest speakers who talk to you about nutrition, diet, and health issues.

Resource Person's Name _____

Title _____

Information about Diet and Nutrients

Nutrition and Health

_____
_____
_____

Health in the Community

_____
_____
_____

Information about Food Production

Foods Produced Locally

_____
_____
_____

Foods Brought in from Outside the Region

_____
_____
_____

Learn from Role Models in the Community 139

ACTIVITY SHEET

Name _____

NOTES ON NUTRITION, DIET, AND HEALTH (part 2)

Transportation Issues

_____
_____
_____
_____
_____
_____
_____

Ideas for Further Investigation

_____
_____
_____
_____
_____
_____
_____

Questions

_____
_____
_____
_____
_____
_____
_____

ACTIVITY SHEET

Name _____

CAMPUS FOOD SERVICE FEATURES (part 1)

Fill in the chart below with information about where food is served on campus and where it comes from. Include information about cost and any nutrition notes you can add as you tour the campus.

Plan for Campus Food Service Audit

Location	Food	Source (vendors; ingredients for on-site preparation)	Cost and Packaging	Nutrition Notes

Tour the School Campus 141

CAMPUS FOOD SERVICE FEATURES (part 2)

Plan for Campus Food Service Audit

Location	Food	Source (vendors; ingredients for on-site preparation)	Cost and Packaging	Nutrition Notes

ACTIVITY SHEET

CAMPUS AUDIT PLAN (part 1)

Name _____ Action Group _____

Complete the following chart to record your plan for auditing campus food service sites.

Plan for Campus Food Service Audit

Study Area/ Types of Food	Notes about Food Preparation, Vendors, Packaging	Action Group (Student Names)	Permission Required/ Accessibility	Audit Due Date

Prepare Your Audit 143

ACTIVITY SHEET — ANALYZE

Name _____

Action Group _____

CAMPUS AUDIT PLAN (part 2)

Plan for Campus Food Service Audit

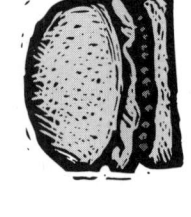

Study Area/ Types of Food	Notes about Food Preparation, Vendors, Packaging	Action Group (Student Names)	Permission Required/ Accessibility	Audit Due Date

144 Prepare Your Audit

© The Tides Center/E2: Environment & Education

ACTIVITY SHEET

Name _____ Action Group _____

DETAILS OF STUDY AREA (part 1)

Look at the foods served in your study area.
Record details of your observations in the chart below.
Then, in part 2, assign food choices to sections of the Food Guide Pyramid.

Food Choices	How Foods Are Prepared	Ingredients	Food and/or Packaging Waste

Conduct Your Audit 145

ACTIVITY SHEET

Name _____   Action Group _____

DETAILS OF STUDY AREA (part 2)

The Food Guide Pyramid
A Guide to Daily Food Choices

KEY
- Fat (naturally occurring and added)
- ▼ Sugars (added)

These symbols show fat and added sugars in foods.

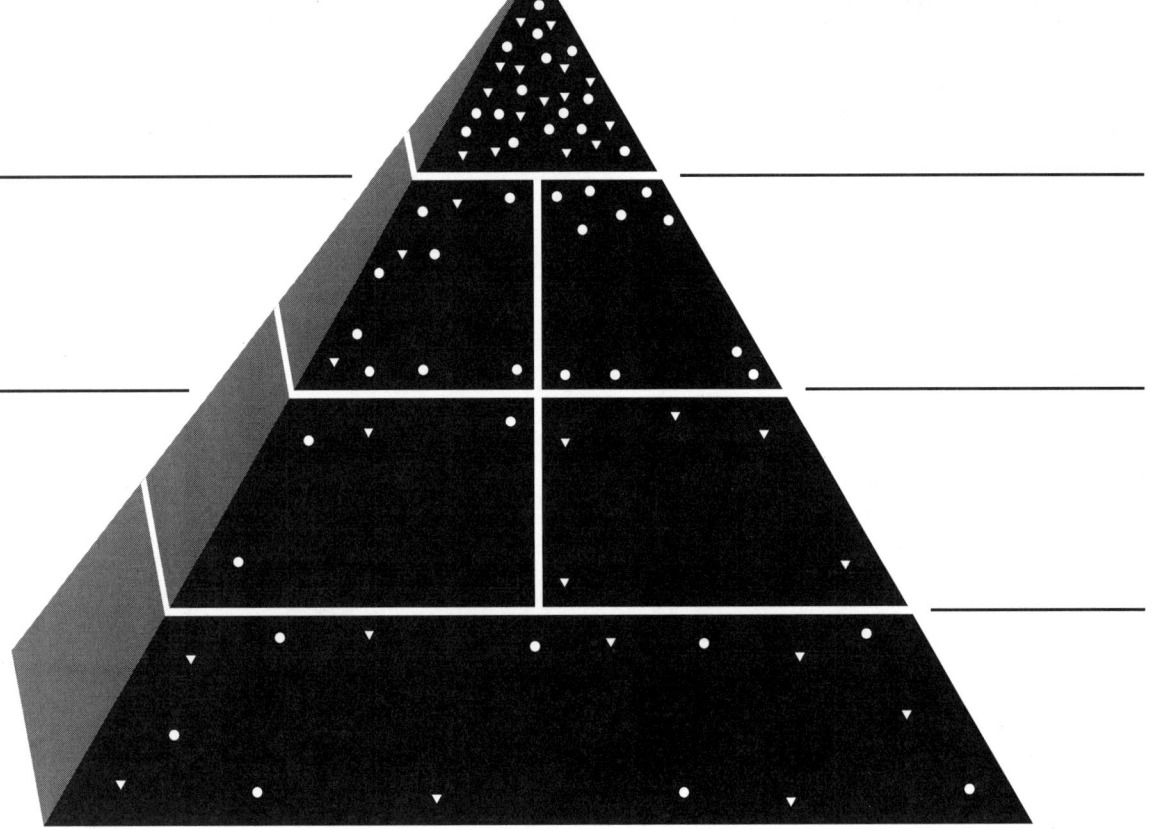

Source: U.S. Department of Agriculture/U.S. Department of Health and Human Services

Name: _____

ACTIVITY SHEET 9 — ANALYZE

FOOD DATA SHEET

Use the following chart to collect information about the foods served in your assigned area.

FOOD CHOICES	NUTRIENTS

Research Ingredients in Food Choices 147

ACTIVITY SHEET

CAMPUS FOOD SERVICE (Part 1)

Name _____

Action Group _____

Combine the audit results from all Action Groups on the chart below.

Foods Served at All Study Areas

Food Choices	Nutritional Value	Waste (Packaging and Uneaten Food)	Notes

ACTIVITY SHEET

Name

Action Group

CAMPUS FOOD SERVICE (Part 2)

Foods Served at All Study Areas

Food Choices	Nutritional Value	Waste (Packaging and Uneaten Food)	Notes

Summarize Findings

ACTIVITY SHEET

Name _____

EVALUATION SHEET (part 1)

Use the following chart to help organize your ideas as you evaluate which food choices are healthy for the environment and for the body at each study area. Use your notes and information on Activity Sheets 9 and 10, as well as what you have learned from the nutrient chart and Food Guide Pyramid. Fill out a sheet for each study area.

Study Area: _____

Food Choices

Main Dish	Side Dish	Dessert	Drink	Snack

Healthy Choices for the Body

Main Dish	Side Dish	Dessert	Drink	Snack

150 Evaluate Food Choices

© The Tides Center/E2: Environment & Education

ACTIVITY SHEET

Name _____

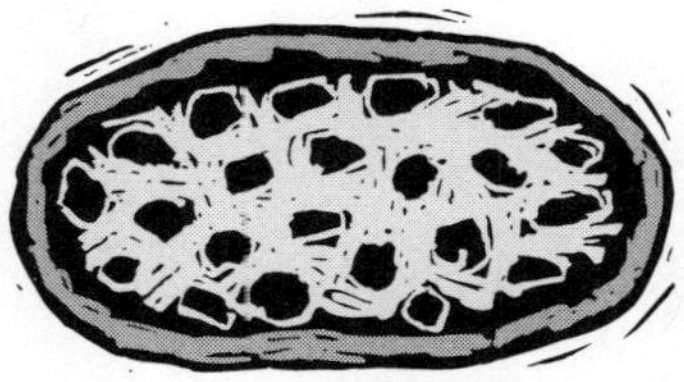

EVALUATION SHEET (part 2)

Healthy Choices for the Environment

Main Dish	Side Dish	Dessert	Drink	Snack

Notes

Evaluate Food Choices 151

ACTIVITY SHEET 12
CONSIDER OPTIONS

Name _____

ASSESSING COSTS AND BENEFITS

Use the following chart to evaluate each healthy food choice you made on Activity Sheet 11.

	Costs	Benefits
Healthy Food Choices for the Body	Monetary: Nonmonetary:	Monetary: Nonmonetary:
Healthy Choices for the Environment	Monetary: Nonmonetary:	Monetary: Nonmonetary:

ACTIVITY SHEET 13
CONSIDER OPTIONS

Name

CHANGING FOOD HABITS (part 1)

Use the chart below to outline how you will change your habits in the food choices you make, taking into account health, the environment, and the costs and benefits of each change. Include notes about changes you would like to see.

Food Choices	For Me	For the School
Main Dishes		
Side Dishes		

Consider Food Choices and Changes 153

ACTIVITY SHEET

Name _____

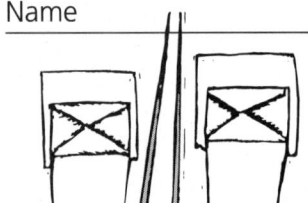

CHANGING FOOD HABITS (part 2)

Food Choices	For Me	For the School
Desserts		
Drinks		
Snacks		

ACTIVITY SHEET

Name

RATING SHEET

Fill in the following rating sheet for each presentation.

Group

Plan

Costs

Expensive •   •   • Inexpensive

Health and Environmental Benefits

Low •   •   • High

Long-Term Effectiveness

Low •   •   • High

Difficulty of Implementing

Low •   •   • High

Cooperation Incentives

Low •   •   • High

Effectiveness of Presentation

Low •   •   • High

Additional Factors to Consider

_____
_____
_____

Priority

Low •   •   • High

PROPOSAL CHECKLIST (part 1)

Use this checklist to plan and monitor tasks that may need to be done in order to complete your proposal. Make a note of who is responsible for completing each task, when each task should be completed, materials needed, and so on. Add to the list as needed.

TASKS	NOTES
1. TITLE ☐ Cover illustration ☐ Proposal statement	
2. WRITE THE INTRODUCTORY PARAGRAPH. ☐ Explain the project. ☐ Briefly describe audit results.	
3. WRITE YOUR RECOMMENDATIONS. ☐ Describe your plan. ☐ Highlight the benefits. ☐ Specify the costs. ☐ Suggest a step-by-step implementation schedule. ☐ Include ideas for motivating student body, increasing awareness, and encouraging participation (if applicable).	

Continue your recommendations on next page.

ACTIVITY SHEET

Name _____

 PROPOSAL CHECKLIST (part 2)

TASKS	NOTES
(CONTINUED)	
4. PRESENT YOUR RESEARCH FINDINGS. ☐ Prepare graphs. ☐ Design tables or charts. ☐ Prepare illustrations, photographs, or other art works.	
5. WRITE YOUR CLOSING STATEMENT. ☐ Outline aspects of the proposal that are already underway and explain where you go from here.	

ACTIVITY SHEET 16 Take Action

Name _____

TRACKING SHEET (part 1)

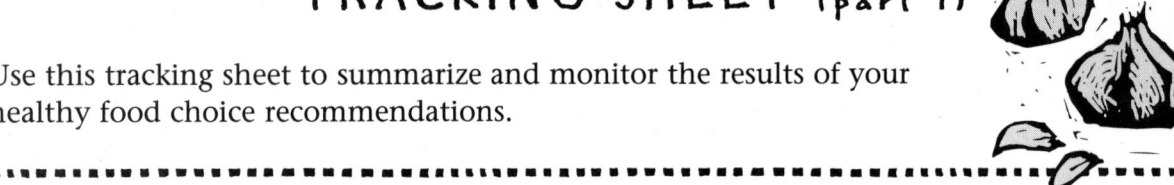

Use this tracking sheet to summarize and monitor the results of your healthy food choice recommendations.

Recommendation

Implementation Report

Month 1

Month 2

ACTIVITY SHEET

Name

TRACKING SHEET (part 2)

Month 3

Participation Rating

Low •   •   • High

Impact on Personal Food Choices

Low •   •   • High

Recommended Changes or Modifications

Name _____

CONTENT QUIZ (part 1)

Circle the correct answer for each question.

1. Some of the environmental problems associated with food production include
    a. soil erosion
    b. desertification
    c. loss of habitat and biodiversity
    d. all of the above

2. The U.S. government does not require packaged and processed foods to have ingredient lists and specific nutrition information on labels.
    a. true   b. false

3. "Eating lower on the food chain" means
    a. eating more dairy products
    b. eating more eggs
    c. eating fewer animal products
    d. eating fewer fruits

4. The diet that is healthiest for the environment is healthiest for people, too.
    a. true   b. false

5. The Food Guide Pyramid recommends that fats and sugars be eaten
    a. once a day
    b. with vegetables
    c. at every meal
    d. sparingly

6. 5-A-Day refers to
    a. servings of fruits and vegetables
    b. number of meals per day
    c. glasses of water per day
    d. slices of bread per day

7. The energy stored in food is measured in
    a. cups
    b. grams
    c. calories
    d. ounces

Name _____

CONTENT QUIZ (part 2)

8. A healthy diet is low in fat, saturated fat, and cholesterol.
    - **a.** true
    - **b.** false

9. The components in food that provide energy and building materials are called
    - **a.** oxidants
    - **b.** nutrients
    - **c.** saturated fats
    - **d.** prototypes

10. Foods closer to the base of the Food Guide Pyramid should be eaten in greatest quantity.
    - **a.** true
    - **b.** false

11. Compare to foods derived from plants, production of foods derived from animals requires
    - **a.** more land
    - **b.** more water
    - **c.** more energy resources
    - **d.** all of the above

12. Most foods do not contain sodium.
    - **a.** true
    - **b.** false

Name _____

STUDENT SURVEY

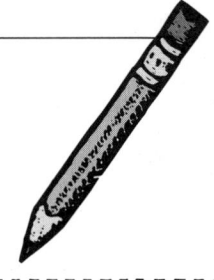

There are no correct answers to the questions below. Answer "yes" or "no."

- -

    YES NO

1. ☐ ☐   I know where the foods I eat come from.

2. ☐ ☐   I understand the environmental impact of food production.

3. ☐ ☐   I try to eat foods that are healthy and nutritious.

4. ☐ ☐   When I make food choices, I am aware of wasted packaging.

5. ☐ ☐   I try to limit the amount of fried, fatty foods I eat.

6. ☐ ☐   I drink at least 6 glasses of water every day.

7. ☐ ☐   I can name the food groups in the Food Guide Pyramid.

8. ☐ ☐   I eat at least 5 servings of fruits and vegetables each day.

9. ☐ ☐   I understand what it means to "eat lower on the food chain."

10. ☐ ☐   I know how my body gets and uses the nutrients it needs.

Name _____ Date _____

Action Group _____

STUDENT SELF-EVALUATION FORM

Evaluate your contributions to Action Group and class activities.

Poor	Average	Good	Excellent

Actively participated in Action Group/class discussions.
Demonstrated a clear understanding of issues.
Took responsibility for research and other tasks.
Provided suggestions and solutions to problems.

How could I have improved my participation in this project? _____
_____
_____

What skills did I improve upon? _____
_____

Which need further improvement? _____
_____

As a result of participating in this project:

What new knowledge have you gained? Have you shared knowledge with others at school?
_____
_____

How has your opinion about environmental issues/problems changed? _____
_____

Have you made any changes in your daily life and/or home? _____
_____
_____

Assessment Tools

Action Group _____

Date _____ Time _____

ACTION GROUP EVALUATION FORM

Behavioral Functions	Participants' Names				
1. Initiating discussion					
2. Sharing information					
3. Seeking information					
4. Giving opinions					
5. Seeking opinions					
6. Evaluating information					
7. Clarifying information					
8. Dramatizing points					
9. Coordinating tasks					
10. Finding compromises					
11. Suggesting procedures					
12. Recording information					
13. Finding middle ground					
14. Relieving tension					
15. Finding norms					
16. Withdrawing from group					
17. Blocking discussion					
18. Seeking recognition					
19. Horsing around					
20. Advocating for group members					
21. Dominating discussion					
22. Criticizing others					

(Adapted from *Effective Group Discussion*, 4th edition, by John K. Brilhart, Wm. C. Brown Company Publishers, Dubuque, IA)

PROGRAM EVALUATION FORM (part 1)

Teachers: In an effort to continually upgrade this module, we are asking for constructive criticism and suggestions for improvement. Please complete an evaluation form for each module and return to:

E2: Environment & Education
P.O. Box 20515
Boulder, CO 80308-3515
303/442-3339 Fax: 303/442-6633
email: e2ee@enviroaction.org

Name _____

School _____

School address _____

Grade(s) taught _____

1. Please check the module(s) that you used:
   ☐ Energy Conservation   ☐ Water Conservation   ☐ Waste Reduction
   ☐ Food Choices   ☐ Habitat and Biodiversity   ☐ Chemicals: Choosing Wisely

2. What did you like most about the module(s)?
   _____
   _____
   _____

3. What did you like least about the module(s)?
   _____
   _____
   _____

4. Please comment on the following aspects of the modules:
   Readability
   _____
   _____

   Instructions
   _____
   _____

   Organization
   _____
   _____

   Graphics and Layout
   _____

Assessment Tools   165

Name _____

PROGRAM EVALUATION FORM (part 2)

Readability
_____
_____

Instructions
_____
_____

Organization
_____
_____
_____

5. Rate how the module affected your students' environmental awareness.

	Not at all				Very much so
Awareness of issues	1	2	3	4	5
Knowledge of issues	1	2	3	4	5
Sense of responsibility	1	2	3	4	5
Sense of ability to effect change	1	2	3	4	5

6. Rate the overall involvement of the following groups in conducting and implementing environmental activities at your school.

	Not at all				Enthusiastically
Students	1	2	3	4	5
Maintenance Staff	1	2	3	4	5
School Administrators	1	2	3	4	5
Parents	1	2	3	4	5
Teachers	1	2	3	4	5
Local Community Organizations	1	2	3	4	5
Local Businesses	1	2	3	4	5
Others _____	1	2	3	4	5